Best Garden Plants *for* Pennsylvania

Ilene Sternberg
Alison Beck

Lone Pine Publishing International

The Distributor: Lone Pine Publishing
1808 B Street NW, Suite 140
Auburn, WA, USA 98001

Website: www.lonepinepublishing.com

Library and Archives Canada Cataloguing in Publication

Sternberg, Ilene
 Best garden plants for Pennsylvania / Ilene Sternberg, Alison Beck.

Includes index.
ISBN–13: 978–1–55105–522–0
ISBN–10: 1–55105–522–8

 1. Plants, Ornamental—Pennsylvania. 2. Gardening—Pennsylvania.
I. Beck, Alison, 1971– II. Title.

SB453.2.P4S84 2006   635.9'09748   C2005–906265–7

Scanning & Electronic Film: Elite Lithographers Co.

Photography: all photos by **Tim Matheson, Tamara Eder, Laura Peters** and **Allison Penko** except: **Sandra Bit** 89a; **Conard-Pyle Roses** 120a; **Janet Davis** (11) 75b; **Joan de Grey** 45a; **Therese D'Monte** 140b; **Don Doucette** 105a&b; **Jen Fafard** 137a; **Derek Fell** 44b, 110a, 120, 140a; **Erika Flatt** 9b, 87a, 106b, 133b, 139a, 164b; **Anne Gordon** 129b; **Lynne Harrison** 99a; **Saxon Holt** 110b, 140b; **Horticolor** (G4500059) 124b, (N0400122)129a; **Dawn Loewen** 65a, 71a; **Kim Patrick O'Leary** 69a, 135a, 148b; **Duncan Kelbaugh** 133a; **Liz Klose** 167a&b; **Marilynn McAra** 137b, 138b; **Photos.com** 45b, 138a, 142a; **Robert Ritchie** 48a&b, 94a, 115a, 118a, 125a; **Leila Sidi** 142b; **Joy Spurr** 124a; **Peter Thompstone** 18a, 26a, 50a, 59b, 61a; **Mark Turner** 75a, 77a; **Baldo Villegas** (President, Sierra Foothills Rose Society; Member, Sacramento Rose Society) 119; **Don Williamson** 59a, 134a&b.

Front cover photographs by Tim Matheson *and* Tamara Eder, *except where noted (clockwise from top right corner)*: Golden Celebration rose, iris, lilac, daylily, sweet potato vine, daylily (Alison Penko), lily (Laura Peters), dahlia, lily (Erika Flatt), flowering crabapple.

This book is not intended as a 'how-to' guide for eating garden plants. Do not consume any plant or plant extract unless you are certain of its identity and toxicity and of your potential for allergic reactions.

RC.P13

Table of Contents

Happy Birthday Nancy and Bob

P.S. you probably know all this but I was thinking how beautiful the garden around your house!

Introduction

Starting a garden can seem like a daunting task, but it is also an exciting and rewarding adventure. With so many plants to choose from, the challenge is deciding which ones and how many you can include in your garden. This book is intended to give beginning gardeners the information they need to start planning and planting gardens of their own. It describes a wide variety of plants and provides planting and growing information and tips for getting you started producing a beautiful and functional landscape.

Pennsylvania has a temperate climate; the summer growing season is long and warm, and the winters are cold enough to ensure a good period of dormancy and plenty of flowers in spring. Rainfall is fairly predictable and the soil, though not without its challenges, supports a variety of healthy plants.

Hardiness zones and frost dates are two terms often used when discussing climate and gardening. Hardiness zones are based on the minimum possible winter temperatures. Plants are rated based on the zones in which they grow successfully. The last-frost date in spring combined with the first-frost date in fall allows us to predict the length of the growing season and gives us an idea of when we can begin planting out in spring.

Microclimates are small areas that are generally warmer or colder than the surrounding area. Buildings, fences, trees and other large structures can provide extra shelter in winter but may trap heat in summer, thus creating a warmer microclimate. The bottoms of hills are usually colder than the tops but may not be as windy. Take advantage of these areas when you plan your garden and choose your plants; you may even grow out-of-zone plants successfully in a warm, sheltered location.

Getting Started

When planning your garden, start with a quick analysis of the garden as it is now. Plants have different requirements, and it is best to put the right plant in the right place rather than to try to change your garden to suit the plants you want.

Knowing which parts of your garden receive the most and least amounts of sunlight will help you choose the proper plants and decide where to plant them. Light is classified into four basic groups: full sun (direct, unobstructed light all or most of the day); partial shade (direct sun for about half the day and shade for the rest); light shade (shade all or most of the day with some sun filtering through to ground level); and full shade (no direct sunlight). Most plants prefer a certain amount of light, but many can adapt to a range of light levels.

The soil is the foundation of a good garden. Plants use the soil to hold themselves upright, but also rely on the many resources it holds: air, water, nutrients, organic matter and a host of microbes. The particle size of the soil influences the amount of air, water and nutrients it can hold. Sand, with the largest particles, has lots of air space and allows water and nutrients to drain quickly. Clay, with the smallest particles, is high in nutrients but has very little air space. Water is therefore slow to penetrate clay and slow to drain from it.

Soil acidity or alkalinity (measured on the pH scale) influences the amount and type of nutrients available to plants. A pH of 7 is neutral; a lower pH is more acidic. Most plants prefer a soil with a pH of 5.5–7.5. Soil-testing kits are available at most garden centers, and soil samples can be sent to testing facilities for a more thorough analysis. This will give you an idea of what plants will do well in your soil and what amendments might need to be made to your soil.

Compost is one of the best and most important amendments you can add to any type of soil. Compost improves soil by adding organic matter and nutrients, introducing soil microbes, increasing water retention and improving drainage. Compost can be purchased or you can make it in your own backyard.

Average Annual Minimum Temperature	
4	- 0 to -25
5a	-15 to -20
5b	-10 to -15
6a	-5 to -10
6b	0 to -5
7a	5 to 0
7b	10 to 5

Hardiness Zones Map

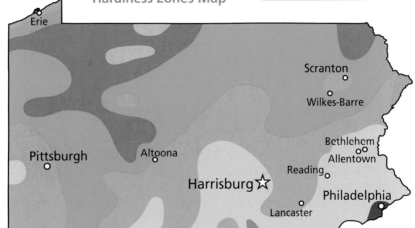

Selecting Plants

It's important to purchase healthy plants that are free of pests and diseases. Such plants will establish quickly in your garden and won't introduce problems that may spread to other plants. You should have a good idea of what the plant is supposed to look like—the color and shape of the leaves and the habit of the plant—and then inspect the plant for signs of disease or insect damage.

The majority of plants are container grown. This is an efficient way for nurseries and greenhouses to grow plants, but when plants grow in a restricted space for too long, they can become pot bound with their roots densely encircling the inside of the pot. Avoid purchasing plants in this condition; they are often stressed and can take longer to establish. It is often possible to remove pots temporarily to look at the condition of the roots. You can check for soil-borne insects, rotten roots and girdling or pot-bound roots at the same time. Roots wrapping densely around the inside of a pot must be lightly pruned or teased apart before planting.

Planting Basics

The following tips apply to all plants.

• Prepare the garden before planting. Remove weeds, make any needed amendments and dig or till the soil in preparation for planting if you are starting a new landscape. This may be more difficult in established beds to which you want to add a single plant. The prepared area should be the size of the plant's mature root system.

• Settle the soil with water. Good contact between the roots and the soil is important, but if you press the soil down too firmly, as often happens when you step on the soil, you can cause compaction, which reduces the movement of water through the soil and leaves very few air spaces. Instead, pour water in as you fill the hole with soil. The water will settle the soil evenly without allowing it to compact.

• Unwrap the roots. It is always best to remove any container before planting to give roots the chance to spread out naturally when planted. In particular, you should remove plastic containers, fiber pots, wire and burlap before planting trees. Fiber pots decompose very slowly, if at all, and wick moisture away from the plant. Burlap may be synthetic, which won't decompose, and wire can eventually strangle the roots as they mature. The only exceptions to this rule are the peat pots and pellets used to start annuals and vegetables; these decompose and can be planted with the young transplants. Even these peat pots should be sliced down the sides and any of the pot that will be exposed above ground removed to prevent water from being wicked away from the roots.

Gently remove container.

Ensure proper planting depth.

Backfill with soil.

- Accommodate the rootball. If you prepared your planting spot ahead of time so it will accommodate the mature roots, your planting hole will only need to be big enough to accommodate the rootball with the roots spread out slightly.

- Know the mature size. Plant based on how big plants will grow rather than how big they are when you plant them. Large plants should have enough room to mature without interfering with walls, roof overhangs, power lines, walkways and surrounding plants.

- Plant at the same depth. Plants generally like to grow at a certain level in relation to the soil and should be planted at the same level they were at in the pot or container before you transplanted them.

- Identify your plants. Keep track of what's what in your garden by putting a tag next to each plant when you plant it. A gardening journal is also a great place to list the plants you have and where you planted them. It is very easy for beginning and seasoned gardeners alike to forget exactly what they planted and where they planted it.

- Water deeply. It's better to water deeply once every week or two, depending on the plant, rather than to water a little bit more often. Deep and thorough watering forces roots to grow as they search for water and helps them survive dry spells when water bans may restrict your watering regime. Always check the rootzone before you water as some soils hold more water for longer than other soils. More gardeners overwater than underwater. Mulching helps retain moisture and reduces watering needs. Containers are the watering exception as they can quickly dry out and may even need watering every day.

Choosing Plants

When choosing the plants, aim for a variety of sizes, shapes, textures, features and bloom times. Features like decorative fruit, variegated or colorful leaves and interesting bark provide interest when plants aren't blooming. This way you will have a garden that captivates your attention all year.

Annuals

Annuals are planted new each year and are only expected to last for a single growing season. Their flowers and decorative foliage provide bright splashes of color and can fill in spaces around immature trees, shrubs and perennials.

Annuals are easy to plant and are usually sold in small cell-packs of four or six. The roots quickly fill the space in these small packs, so the small rootball should be broken up before planting. You can often split the ball in two up the center, or run your thumb up each side to break up the roots.

Settle backfilled soil with water.

Water the plant well.

Add a layer of mulch.

Many annuals are grown from seed and can be started directly in the garden once the soil begins to warm up.

Perennials

Perennials grow for three or more years. They usually die back to the ground each fall and send up new shoots in spring, though they can also be evergreen or semi-shrubby. They often have a shorter period of bloom than annuals but require less care.

Many perennials benefit from being divided every few years, usually in early spring while plants are still dormant or, in some cases, after flowering. This keeps them growing and blooming vigorously, and in some cases controls their spread. Dividing involves digging the plant up, removing dead debris, breaking the plant into several pieces using a sharp knife, spade or saw and replanting some or all of the pieces. Extra pieces can be shared with family, friends and neighbors.

Trees & Shrubs

Trees and shrubs provide the bones of the garden. They are often the slowest growing plants but usually live the

Roses are lovely on their own or in mixed borders.

longest. Characterized by leaf type, they may be deciduous or evergreen, and needled or broad-leaved.

Trees should have as little disturbed soil as possible at the bottom of the planting hole. Loose dirt settles over time and sinking even an inch can kill some trees. The prepared area for trees and shrubs needs to be at least two to four times bigger than the rootball.

Staking, sometimes recommended for newly planted trees, is only necessary for trees over 5' tall. Stakes support the rootball until it grows enough to support the tree. Stakes should allow the trunk to move with the wind.

Pruning is more often required for shrubs than trees. It helps them maintain an attractive shape and can improve blooming.

Roses

Roses are beautiful shrubs with lovely, often fragrant blooms. Traditionally, most roses only bloomed once in the growing season, but new varieties bloom all, or almost all, summer. Repeat

Trees and shrubs provide backbone to the mixed border.

Training vines to climb arbors adds structure to the garden.

Lilies bloom throughout summer.

blooming, or recurrent, roses should be deadheaded to encourage more flower production. One-time bloomers should be left for the colorful hips that develop.

Generally, roses prefer a fertile, well-prepared planting area. A rule of thumb is to prepare an area 24" across, front to back and side to side, and 24" deep. Add plenty of compost or other fertile organic matter, and keep roses well watered during the growing season. Many roses are quite durable and will adapt to poorer conditions. Grafted roses should be planted with the graft two inches below the soil line. When watering, avoid getting water on the foliage to reduce the spread of blackspot.

Vines

Vines or climbing plants are useful for screening and shade, especially in a location too small for a tree. They may be woody or herbaceous, and annual or perennial. Vines may physically cling to surfaces, may have wrapping tendrils or stems or may need to be tied in place with string.

Sturdy trellises, arbors, porch railings, fences, walls, poles and trees are all possible vine supports. If a support is needed, ensure it's in place before you plant to avoid disturbing the roots later. Choose a support that is suitable for the vine you are growing. It needs to be sturdy enough to hold the plant up and should match the growing habit—clinging, wrapping or tied—of the vine.

Bulbs, Corms, Tubers

These plants have fleshy underground storage organs that allow them to survive extended periods of dormancy. They are often grown for the bright splashes of color their flowers provide. They may be spring, summer or fall flowering. Each has an ideal depth and time of year at which it should be planted.

Hardy bulbs can be left in the ground and will flower every year. Some popular tender plants are grown from bulbs, corms or tubers and are generally lifted from the garden in late summer or fall as the foliage dies back. These are stored in a cool, frost-free location for winter, to be replanted in spring.

Many herbs grow well in pots.

Herbs

Herbs are plants with medicinal, culinary or other economic purposes. A few common culinary herbs are included in this book. Even if you don't cook with them, the often-fragrant foliage adds its aroma to the garden, and the plants can be quite decorative in form, leaf and flower. A conveniently placed container—perhaps near the kitchen door—of your favorite herbs will yield plenty of flavor and fragrance all summer.

Ornamental grasses add color, variety and texture.

Many herbs have pollen-producing flowers that attract butterflies, bees, hummingbirds and predatory insects to your garden. Predatory insects feast on problem insects such as aphids, mealy bugs and whiteflies.

Foliage Plants

Many plants are grown for their decorative foliage rather than their flowers, which may also be decorative. Many of these are included in other sections of this book, but we have set aside a few for the unique touch their foliage adds to the garden.

Ornamental grasses and grass-like plants offer a variety of forms, textures and foliage colors and provide interest all year when the withered blades are left to stand all winter. They are cut back in early spring and divided when the clumps begin to die out in the centers.

Ferns provide a lacy foliage accent and combine attractively with broad-leaved perennials and shrubs. A common sight in moist and shady gardens, there are also ferns that will survive in full sun.

A Final Comment

The more you discover about the fascinating world of plants, whether it be from reading books, talking to other gardeners, appreciating the creative designs of others, or experimenting with something new in your own garden, the more rewarding your gardening experience will be. This book is intended as a guide to germinate and grow your passion for plants.

Angelonia

Angelonia

A. *angustifolia* 'Alba' (above), A. *angustifolia* 'Blue Pacific' (below)

With its loose, airy spikes of orchid-like flowers, angelonia makes a welcome addition to the garden.

Growing

Angelonia prefers **full sun** but tolerates a bit of shade. The soil should be **fertile, moist** and **well drained**. Although this plant grows naturally in damp areas, such as along ditches and near ponds, it is fairly drought tolerant. Plant out after the chance of frost has passed.

Tips

Angelonia makes a good addition to an annual or mixed border where it is most attractive when planted in groups. It is also suited to a pondside or streamside planting.

Recommended

A. angustifolia is a bushy, upright plant with loose spikes of flowers in varied shades of purple. Cultivars with white or bicolored flowers are available.

The individual flowers look a bit like orchid blossoms, but angelonia is actually in the same family as snapdragon.

Also called: angel wings, summer snapdragon
Features: attractive, purple, blue, white, bicolored flowers **Height:** 12–24" **Spread:** 12"

Bacopa
Sutera

S. cordata (above & below)

Bacopa is a perennial that is grown as an annual outdoors. It will thrive as a houseplant in a bright room.

Bacopa snuggles under and around the stems of taller plants, forming a dense carpet dotted with tiny, white to pale lavender flowers, and eventually drifts over pot edges to form a waterfall of stars.

Growing
Bacopa grows well in **partial shade**, with protection from the hot afternoon sun. The soil should be of **average fertility, humus rich, moist** and **well drained**. Don't allow this plant to dry out, or the leaves will quickly die. Cutting back dead growth may encourage new shoots to form.

Tips
Bacopa is a popular plant for hanging baskets, mixed containers and window boxes. It is not recommended as a bedding plant because it fizzles quickly when the weather gets hot, particularly if you forget to water. Plant it where you will see it every day so you will remember to water it.

Recommended
S. cordata is a compact, trailing plant that bears small, white flowers all summer. Cultivars with larger, white or lavender flowers, or gold and green variegated foliage are available.

Features: decorative, white or lavender flowers; foliage; habit **Height:** 3–6" **Spread:** 12–20"

Begonia
Begonia

With its beautiful flowers, compact habit and decorative foliage, there is sure to be a begonia to fulfill your shade gardening needs.

Growing
Light or partial shade is best, though some wax begonias tolerate sun if the soil is kept moist. The soil should be **fertile, rich in organic matter** and **well drained** with a **neutral or acidic pH**. Allow the soil to dry out slightly between waterings, particularly for tuberous begonias. Begonias love warm weather, so don't plant them before the soil warms in spring. If they sit in cold soil, they may become stunted and fail to thrive.

Tips
All begonias are useful for shaded garden beds and planters. The trailing tuberous varieties can be used in hanging baskets and along rock walls where the flowers will cascade over the edges. Wax begonias have a neat, rounded habit that makes them particularly attractive as edging plants. Rex begonias, with their dramatic foliage, are useful as specimen plants in containers and beds.

Recommended
B. Rex Cultorum **Hybrids** (rex begonias) are grown for their dramatic, colorful foliage.

B. semperflorens (wax begonias) have pink, white, red or bicolored flowers and

B. Rex Cultorum 'Escargot' (above)
B. x *tuberhybrida* (below)

green, bronze, reddish or white-variegated foliage.

B. x *tuberhybrida* (tuberous begonias) are generally sold as tubers and are popular for their flowers that grow in many shades of red, pink, yellow, orange or white.

Features: pink, white, red, yellow, orange, bicolored, picotee flowers; decorative foliage
Height: 6–24" **Spread:** 6–24"

Black-Eyed Susan
Rudbeckia

R. hirta 'Becky Mixed' (above), *R. hirta* (below)

Black-eyed Susan brightens up any spot in the garden, and its tolerance for heavy soils makes it useful in new developments where the topsoil is often very thin.

Growing
Black-eyed Susan grows equally well in **full sun** or **partial shade**. The soil should be of **average fertility, humus rich, moist** and **well drained**. This plant tolerates heavy clay soil and hot weather. If it is growing in loose, moist soil, black-eyed Susan may reseed itself.

Black-eyed Susan makes a long-lasting vase flower.

Plants can be purchased, started from seed early indoors or directly sown in the garden around the last frost date. Deadhead to prolong blooming.

Tips
Plant black-eyed Susan individually or in groups. Use it in beds and borders, large containers, meadow plantings and wildflower gardens. This plant will bloom well, even in the hottest part of the garden.

Recommended
R. hirta forms a bristly mound of foliage and bears bright yellow, daisy-like flowers with brown centers in summer and fall. A wide variety of cultivars are available, including dwarf plants and double-flowered plants.

Perennial black-eyed Susans are also available but can become invasive.

Also called: coneflower **Features:** yellow, orange, red, brown, sometimes bicolored flowers; brown or green centers
Height: 8–36" or more **Spread:** 12–18"

Calendula
Calendula

Calendulas are bright and charming, producing attractive flowers in warm colors all summer and fall.

Growing

Calendula does equally well in **full sun** or **partial shade**. It likes cool weather and can withstand a moderate frost. The soil should be of **average fertility** and **well drained**. Deadhead to prolong blooming and keep plants looking neat.

If plants fade in summer heat, cut them back to 4–6" above the ground to promote new growth, or pull them up and seed new ones. Either method will provide a good fall display. Sow seed directly into the garden in mid-spring.

Tips

This informal plant looks attractive in borders and mixed into a vegetable patch. It can also be used in mixed planters. Calendula is a cold-hardy annual and often continues flowering, even through a layer of snow, until the ground freezes completely.

Recommended

C. officinalis is a vigorous, tough, upright plant that bears daisy-like, single or double flowers in a wide range of yellow and orange shades. Several cultivars are available.

C. *officinalis* 'Apricot Surprise' (above)
C. *officinalis* (below)

Calendula flowers are popular kitchen herbs that can be added to stews for color or to salads for flavoring. They can also be brewed into an infusion that is useful as a wash for minor cuts and bruises.

Also called: pot marigold, English marigold
Features: cream, yellow, gold, orange, apricot flowers; long blooming period
Height: 10–24" **Spread:** 8–20"

California Poppy

Eschscholzia

E. californica (above & below)

The petals of California poppy can be eaten. They have little nutritional value but the color will brighten up a salad.

California poppies are aptly described as the shimmering, fluttering apricot orange jewels of the West.

Growing

California poppy prefers **full sun**. The soil should be of **poor or average fertility** and **well drained**. With too rich a soil, the growth will be lush and green, but the plant will bear few, if any, flowers. This plant is drought tolerant once established, but it requires a lot of water for germination and until it begins flowering.

Never start this plant indoors because it dislikes having its roots disturbed. California poppy will sprout quickly when sown directly in the garden in early to mid-spring.

Tips

California poppy can be included in an annual border or annual planting in a cottage garden. This plant self-seeds wherever it is planted; it is perfect for naturalizing in a meadow garden or rock garden where it will come back year after year.

Recommended

E. californica forms a mound of delicate, feathery, blue-green foliage. It bears satiny, orange or yellow flowers all summer. Cultivars with semi-double or double flowers in red, cream or pink are available.

Features: orange, yellow, red, violet, cream and less commonly pink, flowers; attractive feathery foliage **Height:** 8–18" **Spread:** 8–18"

Cleome

Cleome

C. *hassleriana* (above & below)

Create a bold and exotic display in your garden with these lovely and unusual flowers.

Growing

Cleome prefers **full sun** but tolerates **partial shade**. Plants **adapt to most soils**, though mixing in **organic matter** to help retain water is a good idea. These plants are drought tolerant but perform best when watered regularly. Pinch out the tip of the center stem on young plants to encourage branching and more blooms. Deadhead to prolong blooming and to reduce prolific self-seeding.

Tips

Cleome can be planted in groups at the back or a border or in the center of an island bed. These striking plants also make an attractive addition to a large mixed container planting.

Recommended

C. hassleriana is a tall, upright plant with strong, supple, thorny stems. The foliage and flowers of this plant have a strong but not unpleasant scent. Flowers are borne in loose, rounded clusters at the ends of the leafy stems. Many cultivars are available.

C. serrulata (Rocky Mountain bee plant) is native to western North America but is rarely available commercially. The thornless dwarf cultivar **'Solo'** is regularly available to be grown from seed and grows 12–18" tall with pink and white flowers.

Also called: spider flower **Features:** attractive and scented foliage; purple, pink, white flowers; thorny stems **Height:** 1–5' **Spread:** 12–24"

Fan Flower
Scaevola

S. aemula (above & below)

Fan flower's intriguing one-sided flowers add interest to hanging baskets, planters and window boxes.

Growing
Fan flower grows well in **full sun** or **light shade**. The soil should be of **average fertility, moist** and very **well drained**. Water regularly because this plant doesn't like to dry out completely. It does, however, recover quickly from wilting when watered.

Tips
Fan flower is popular for hanging baskets and containers, but it can also be used along the tops of rock walls and in rock gardens where it will trail down. This plant makes an interesting addition to mixed borders, or it can be used under shrubs, where the long, trailing stems will form an attractive ground-cover.

Recommended
S. aemula forms a mound of foliage from which trailing stems emerge. The fan-shaped flowers come in shades of purple, usually with white bases. The species is rarely grown because there are many improved cultivars.

Given the right conditions, this Australian plant will flower abundantly from April through to frost.

Features: unique, blue or purple flowers; trailing habit **Height:** up to 8" **Spread:** 36" or more

Foxglove
Digitalis

*F*oxgloves are a perfect foil for the members of the daisy family that are so common in the summer landscape.

Growing
Foxgloves grow well in **partial** or **light shade**. The soil should be **fertile, humus rich, acidic** and **moist**. Seeds can be started in mid- to late summer for blooms the following summer, or plants can be purchased in spring that will bloom the summer they are planted. Plants often self-seed and may pop up in your garden in future summers.

Tips
Foxgloves are must-haves for the cottage garden and for gardeners interested in heritage plants. They make excellent vertical accents along the back of the border and are attractive additions to woodland gardens.

Recommended
D. purpurea forms a mounding basal rosette of foliage from which the tall flower spikes emerge. Plants bloom in early summer with flowers in a wide range of colors, often with contrasting speckles on the insides of the flowers. There are many cultivars available.

D. purpurea (above & below)

All parts of this plant are poisonous; wear gloves and wash your hands thoroughly after handling it.

Also called: purple foxglove **Features:** pink, purple, yellow, maroon, red, white early-summer flowers; habit **Height:** 2–5' **Spread:** 12–24"

Gazania
Gazania

G. *rigens* cultivars (above), G. *rigens* (below)

*F*ew other flowers can rival gazania for adding vivid oranges, reds and yellows to the garden.

Growing

Gazania grows best in **full sun** but tolerates some shade. The soil should be of **poor to average fertility, sandy** and **well drained**. Gazania is drought tolerant and grows best when temperatures are over 78°F. Flowers may only stay open on sunny days.

Tips

Low-growing gazania makes an excellent groundcover and is also useful on exposed slopes, in mixed containers and as an edging in flowerbeds. It is a wonderful plant for a xeriscape or dry garden design.

Recommended

G. rigens forms a low basal rosette of lobed foliage. Large, daisy-like flowers with pointed petals are borne on strong stems above the plant. Many cultivars are available.

This native of southern Africa has very few pests and transplants easily, even when blooming.

Features: red, orange, yellow, pink, cream flowers **Height:** usually 6–8"; may grow up to 12–18"
Spread: 8–12"

Geranium
Pelargonium

ough, predictable, sun-loving and drought resistant, geraniums have earned their place as flowering favorites in the annual garden. If you are looking for something out of the ordinary, seek out the scented geraniums with their fragrant and often decorative foliage.

Growing
Geraniums prefer **full sun** but tolerate partial shade, though they may not bloom as profusely. The soil should be **fertile** and **well drained**. Deadheading is essential to keep geraniums blooming and looking neat.

Tips
Geraniums are very popular annual plants, used in borders, beds, planters, hanging baskets and window boxes.

Geraniums are perennials that are treated as annuals and can be kept indoors over winter in a bright room.

Recommended
P. peltatum (ivy-leaved geranium) has thick, waxy leaves and a trailing habit. Many cultivars are available.

P. zonale (zonal geranium) is a bushy plant with red, pink, purple, orange or white flowers and, frequently, banded or multi-colored foliage. Many cultivars are available.

P. **species** and **cultivars** (scented geraniums, scented pelargoniums) is a large group of geraniums that have fragrant leaves. The scents are grouped into categories, including rose, mint, citrus, fruit, spice and pungent.

P. peltatum (above & below)

Ivy-leaved geranium is one of the most beautiful plants to include in a mixed hanging basket.

Features: red, pink, violet, orange, salmon, white, purple flowers; decorative or scented foliage; variable habits
Height: 8–24" **Spread:** 6"–4'

Impatiens
Impatiens

I. walleriana (above), *I. hawkeri* (below)

The English named I. walleriana *busy Lizzie because it flowers continuously through the growing season.*

*I*mpatiens are the high-wattage darlings of the shade garden, delivering masses of flowers in a wide variety of colors.

Growing
Impatiens do best in **partial shade** or **light shade** but tolerate full shade or, if kept moist, full sun. New Guinea impatiens are the best adapted to sunny locations. The soil should be **fertile, humus rich, moist** and **well drained**.

Tips
Impatiens are known for their ability to grow and flower profusely even in shade. Mass plant them in beds under trees, along shady fences or walls or in porch planters. They also look lovely in hanging baskets. New Guinea impatiens are grown as much for their variegated leaves as for their flowers.

Recommended
I. hawkeri (New Guinea Hybrids; New Guinea impatiens) flowers in shades of red, orange, pink, purple or white. The foliage is often variegated with a yellow stripe down the center of each leaf.

I. walleriana (impatiens, busy Lizzie) flowers in shades of purple, red, burgundy, pink, yellow, salmon, orange, apricot, white or can be bicolored. Dozens of cultivars are available.

Also called: busy Lizzie **Features:** flowers in shades of purple, red, burgundy, pink, yellow, salmon, orange, apricot, white, bicolored; grows well in shade **Height:** 6–36" **Spread:** 12–24"

Love-in-a-Mist
Nigella

N. damascena (above & below)

Love-in-a-mist's ferny foliage and delicate, blue flowers blend with most plants. It has a tendency to self-sow and may show up in unexpected spots in your garden for years to come.

Growing

Love-in-a-mist prefers **full sun**. The soil should be of **average fertility, light** and **well drained**.

Direct sow seeds at two-week intervals all spring to prolong the blooming period.

Tips

This attractive, airy plant is often used in mixed beds and borders. The flowers appear to float above the delicate foliage. The blooming may be slow and the plants may die back if the weather gets too hot in summer.

The stems of this plant can be a bit floppy and may benefit from being staked with twiggy branches. Poke the branches into the dirt around the plant when it is young, and the plant will grow up between the twigs.

Recommended

N. damascena forms a loose mound of finely divided foliage. Cultivars are available with a wider variety of flower colors than the blue offered by the species.

The aromatic seeds have been used as a cooking spice and as medicine.

Also called: devil-in-a-bush
Features: feathery foliage, exotic blue, white, pink or purple flowers **Height:** 16–24"
Spread: 8–12"

Madagascar Periwinkle
Catharanthus

C. roseus (above & below)

Madagascar periwinkle is a forgiving annual, tolerant of dry spells, searing sun and city pollution. It exhibits grace under all types of pressure.

Growing
Periwinkle prefers **full sun** but tolerates partial shade. Any **well-drained** soil is fine. This plant tolerates pollution and drought but prefers to be watered regularly. It doesn't like to be too wet or too cold. Avoid planting periwinkle until the soil has warmed because it may fail to thrive if planted in cold or wet soil.

Tips
Periwinkle will do well in the sunniest, warmest part of the garden. Plant it in a bed along an exposed driveway or against the south-facing wall of the house. It can also be used in hanging baskets, in planters and as a temporary groundcover.

Recommended
C. roseus (*Vinca rosea*) forms a mound of strong stems. The flowers are pink, red or white, often with contrasting centers. Many cultivars are available.

One of the best annuals to use in front of homes on busy streets, Madagascar periwinkle will bloom happily despite exposure to exhaust fumes and dust.

Features: attractive foliage; flowers in shades of red, rose, pink, mauve, white, often with contrasting centers; durable plants
Height: 6–24" **Spread:** usually equal to or greater than height

Marigold
Tagetes

From the large, exotic, ruffled flowers of African marigold to the tiny flowers on the low-growing signet marigold, the warm colors and fresh scent of marigolds add a festive touch to the garden.

Growing

Marigolds grow best in **full sun**. The soil should be of **average fertility** and **well drained**. These plants are drought tolerant and hold up well in windy, rainy weather. Sow seed directly in the garden after the chance of frost has passed. Deadhead to prolong blooming and to keep plants tidy.

Tips

Mass planted or mixed with other plants, marigolds make a vibrant addition to beds, borders and container gardens. These plants will thrive in the hottest, driest parts of your garden.

Recommended

There are many cultivars available for all the species. *T. erecta* (African marigold, American marigold, Aztec marigold) is the largest plant with the biggest flowers; *T. patula* (French marigold) is low growing and has a wide range of flower colors; *T. tenuifolia* (signet marigold) has recently become more popular because of its feathery foliage and small, dainty flowers; *T. Triploid Hybrids* (triploid marigold) have been developed by crossing French and African marigolds, which results in plants with huge flowers and compact growth.

T. tenuifolia (above), *T. patula* (below)

Marigolds are often included in vegetable gardens for their reputed insect- and nematode-repelling qualities.

Features: yellow, red, orange, brown, gold, cream, bicolored flowers; fragrant foliage
Height: 6–36" **Spread:** 12–24"

Million Bells
Calibrachoa

*M*illion bells is charming, and given the right conditions, blooms continually during the growing season.

Growing
Million bells prefers **full sun**. The soil should be **fertile, moist** and **well drained**. Although it prefers to be watered regularly, million bells is fairly drought resistant once established. It blooms well into autumn and becomes hardier over summer and as the weather cools.

Tips
Popular for planters and hanging baskets, million bells is also attractive in beds and borders. It grows all summer and needs plenty of room to spread or it will overtake other flowers. Pinch back to keep plants compact.

'Trailing Blue' (above), 'Trailing Pink' (below)

Calibrachoa flowers close at night and on cloudy days.

Recommended
Calibrachoa **Hybrids** have a dense, trailing habit. They bear small flowers that look like petunias, and cultivars are available in a wide range of flower colors.

Also called: calibrachoa, trailing petunia
Features: pink, purple, yellow, red-orange, white, blue flowers; trailing habit
Height: 6–12" **Spread:** up to 24"

Nasturtium
Tropaeolum

These fast-growing, brightly colored flowers are easy to grow, making them popular with beginners and experienced gardeners alike.

Growing
Nasturtiums prefer **full sun** but tolerate some shade. The soil should be of **poor to average fertility, light, moist** and **well drained**. Soil that is too rich or has too much nitrogen fertilizer will result in a lot of leaves and very few flowers. Let the soil drain completely between waterings. Sow directly in the garden once the danger of frost has passed.

Tips
Nasturtiums are used in beds, borders, containers and hanging baskets and on sloped banks. The climbing varieties are grown up trellises or over rock walls or places that need concealing. These plants thrive in poor locations, and they make an interesting addition to plantings on hard-to-mow slopes.

T. *majus* (above), T. *majus* 'Alaska' (below)

The leaves and flowers are edible, adding a peppery flavor to salads.

Recommended
T. majus has a trailing habit, but many of the cultivars have bushier, more refined habits. Cultivars offer differing flower colors or variegated foliage.

Features: red, orange, yellow, burgundy, pink, cream, gold, white, bicolored flowers; attractive foliage; edible leaves and flowers; varied habits **Height:** 12–18" for dwarf varieties; up to 10' for trailing varieties **Spread:** equal to height

Nicotiana
Nicotiana

N. sylvestris & N. x sanderae (above)
N. x sanderae Nicki Series (below)

Nicotianas were originally culti-vated for the wonderful fragrance of the flowers, a feature that, in some cases, has been lost in favor of an expanded selection of flower colors. Fragrant varieties are still available.

Growing
Nicotianas grow equally well in **full sun, light shade** or **partial shade**. The soil should be **fertile,** high in **organic matter, moist** and **well drained**.

Tips
Nicotianas are popular in beds and borders. The dwarf varieties do well in containers.

Do not plant nicotianas near tomatoes because, as members of the same plant family, they share a vulnerability to many of the same diseases.

Nicotiana plants may attract and harbor diseases that will hardly affect them but that can kill tomatoes.

Recommended
N. x *sanderae* (*N. alata* x *N. forgetiana*) is a hybrid from which many brightly colored and dwarf cultivars have been developed.

N. sylvestris grows up to 4' tall and bears white blooms that are fragrant in the evening.

The seeds require light to germinate, so if you start plants from seed, press them into the soil surface but don't cover them.

Also called: flowering tobacco plant
Features: fragrant red, pink, green, yellow, white, purple flowers **Height:** 1–5'
Spread: 12"

Pansy
Viola

V. x wittrockiana cultivars (above & below)

Colorful and cheerful, pansy flowers are a welcome sight in spring after a long, dreary winter.

Growing
Pansies prefer **full sun** but tolerate partial shade. The soil should be **fertile, moist** and **well drained**. Pansies do best when the weather is cool and may die back over the summer. They may rejuvenate in late summer, but it is often easier to pull up faded plants and replace them with new ones in fall. These may very well survive the winter and provide you with flowers again in spring.

Tips
Pansies can be used in beds and borders, and they are popular for mixing in with

spring-flowering bulbs and primroses. They can also be grown in containers.

Recommended
*V. x **wittrockiana*** is a small bushy plant that bears flowers in a wide range of bright and pastel colors, often with markings near the centers of the petals, which give the flowers a face-like appearance.

Pansy petals are edible and make delightful garnishes on salads and desserts.

Features: flowers in bright or pastel shades of blue, purple, red, orange, yellow, pink, white, often bicolored **Height:** 6–12" **Spread:** 6–12"

Pentas

Pentas

*his plant is a welcome addition to the annual garden not only for its pretty flowers, but also because it prefers not to be watered too often—ideal for those gardeners who aren't very diligent about watering.

Growing

Pentas grows best in **full sun**. The soil should be **fertile**, **moist** and **well drained**. Deadhead to encourage continuous flowering and to keep plants looking tidy. Pinch plants to encourage bushy growth.

Tips

Pentas makes a lovely addition to mixed or herbaceous beds and borders. The coarse, dark foliage creates a good background against which brightly colored flowers stand out. They can also be grown in containers, and cuttings taken in late summer can be grown indoors for the winter.

Recommended

P. lanceolata is a subshrub that is grown as an annual. It has an erect or occasionally prostrate habit. Red, pink, purple or white flowers are produced in clusters. Cultivars are available, including **'Avalanche,'** which has white flowers and variegated foliage.

P. lanceolata cultivar (above)
P. lanceolata (below)

These plants are often available in the winter to be grown as houseplants.

Also called: star clusters, Egyptian star
Features: pink, red, purple, white flowers; foliage **Height:** 24–36" **Spread:** 24–36"

Petunia
Petunia

Milliflora type 'Fantasy' (above), Multiflora type (below)

or speedy growth, prolific bloom-ing and ease of care, petunias are hard to beat.

Growing

Petunias prefer **full sun**. The soil should be of **average to rich fertility, light, sandy** and **well drained**. Pinch halfway back in mid-summer to keep plants bushy and to encourage new growth and flowers.

Tips

Use petunias in beds, borders, containers and hanging baskets.

Recommended

P. x *hybrida* is a large group of popular, sun-loving annuals that fall into three categories: **grandifloras** have the largest flowers in the widest range of colors, but they can be damaged by rain; **multifloras** bear more flowers that are smaller and less easily damaged by heavy rain; and **millifloras** have the smallest flowers in the narrowest range of colors, but this type is the most prolific and least likely to be damaged by heavy rain.

Owing to the introduction of many new and exciting cultivars, petunias are once again among the most popular and sought after of the annual garden flowers.

Features: pink, purple, red, white, yellow, coral, blue, bicolored flowers; versatile plants
Height: 6–18"
Spread: 12–24" or wider

Poppy
Papaver

P. nudicaule (above & below)

Growing
Poppies grow best in **full sun**. The soil should be **fertile** and **sandy** with a lot of **organic matter** mixed in. **Good drainage** is essential. Direct sow every two weeks in spring. Mix the tiny seeds with fine sand for even sowing. Do not cover them because the seeds need light for germination. Deadhead to prolong blooming.

Tips
Poppies work well in mixed borders where other plants are slow to fill in. Poppies will fill in empty spaces early in the season, then die back over the summer, leaving room for other plants. They can also be used in rock gardens, and the cut flowers are popular for fresh arrangements.

Recommended
P. nudicaule (Iceland poppy) bears red, orange, yellow, pink or white flowers in spring and early summer.

P. rhoeas (Flanders poppy, field poppy, corn poppy) forms a basal rosette of foliage above which the flowers in a wide range of colors are borne on long stems.

P. somniferum (opium poppy) bears red, pink, white or purple, often showy, single or double flowers. Although propagation of the species is restricted in many countries, because of its narcotic properties, several attractive cultivars have been developed for ornamental use.

oppies seem to have been made to grow in groups. The many flowers swaying in a breeze, with their often-curving stems, seem to be having lively conversations with one another.

Be careful when weeding around faded summer plants; you may accidentally pull up late-summer poppy seedlings.

Also called: Shirley poppy, corn poppy, Flanders poppy **Features:** red, pink, white, purple, yellow, orange flowers **Height:** 2–4' **Spread:** 12"

Portulaca
Portulaca

*F*or a brilliant show in the hottest, driest, poorest, most neglected area of the garden, you can't go wrong with portulaca.

Growing
Portulaca requires **full sun**. The soil should be of **poor fertility, sandy** and **well drained**. To ensure that you will have plants where you want them, start seeds indoors. If you sow directly outdoors, the tiny seeds may get washed away by rain, and the plants will pop up in unexpected places.

Tips
Portulaca is the ideal plant for garden spots that just don't get enough water—under the eaves of the house or in dry, rocky, exposed areas. It is also ideal for people who like baskets hanging from the front porch but forget to water regularly. Portulaca still needs to be watered occasionally. As long as the location is sunny, this plant will do well with minimal care.

P. grandiflora (above & below)

Spacing the plants closely together is not a problem; in fact, the intertwining of the plants and colorful flowers creates an interesting and attractive effect.

Recommended
P. grandiflora forms a bushy mound of succulent foliage. It bears delicate, papery, rose-like flowers profusely all summer. Many cultivars are available, including those that have flowers that stay open on cloudy days.

Also called: moss rose **Features:** drought-resistant summer flowers in shades of red, pink, yellow, white, purple, orange, peach **Height:** 4–8" **Spread:** 6–12" or wider

Salvia
Salvia

S. *splendens* (red) and S. *farinacea* (purple) with purple lobelia (above), S. *viridis* (below)

The salvias should be part of every annual garden. The attractive and varied forms have something to offer every style of garden.

Growing

All salvia plants prefer **full sun** but tolerate light shade. The soil should be **moist** and **well drained** and of **average to rich fertility** with a lot of **organic matter**. To keep plants producing flowers, water often and fertilize monthly.

Tips

Salvias look good grouped in beds and borders and in containers. The flowers are long lasting and make good cut flowers for arrangements.

Recommended

S. argentea (silver sage) is grown for its large, fuzzy, silvery leaves. *S. coccinea* (Texas sage) is a bushy, upright plant that bears whorled spikes of white, pink, blue or purple flowers. *S. farinacea* (mealy cup sage, blue sage) has bright blue flowers clustered along stems powdered with silver. Cultivars are available. *S. splendens* (salvia, scarlet sage) is grown for its spikes of bright red, tubular flowers. Recently, cultivars have become available in white, pink, purple or orange. *S. viridis* (*S. horminium*; annual clary sage) is grown for its colorful pink, purple, blue or white bracts, rather than the tiny flowers within the bracts.

Also called: sage **Features:** red, blue, purple, burgundy, pink, orange, salmon, yellow, cream, white, bicolored summer flowers; attractive foliage **Height:** 8"–4' **Spread:** 8"–4'

Snapdragon
Antirrhinum

Snapdragons are among the most appealing plants. The flower colors are always rich and vibrant, and even the most jaded gardeners are tempted to squeeze open the dragons' mouths.

Growing

Snapdragons prefer **full sun** but tolerate light or partial shade. The soil should be **fertile, rich in organic matter** and **well drained**. These plants prefer a **neutral or alkaline** soil and do not perform as well in acidic soil. Do not cover seeds when sowing because they require light for germination.

To encourage bushy growth, pinch the tips of the young plants. Cut off the flower spikes as they fade to promote further blooming and to prevent the plant from dying back before the end of the season.

Tips

The height of the variety dictates the best place for it in a border—the shortest varieties work well near the front, and the tallest look good in the center or back. The dwarf and medium-height varieties can also be used in planters. A trailing variety does well in hanging baskets.

Recommended

There are many cultivars of *A. majus* available, generally grouped into three size categories: dwarf, medium and giant.

A. majus cultivars (above & below)

Snapdragons are perennial plants that are treated like annuals. Although they won't usually survive the winter here, they will often flower well into fall and may self-seed.

Features: white, cream, yellow, orange, red, maroon, pink, purple, bicolored flowers
Height: 6"–4' **Spread:** 6–24"

Sunflower

Helianthus

H. annuus 'Teddy Bear' (above), *H. annuus* cultivar (below)

Growing

Sunflower grows best in **full sun**. The soil should be of **average fertility, humus rich, moist** and **well drained**.

The annual sunflower is an excellent plant for children to grow. The seeds are big and easy to handle, and they germinate quickly. The plants grow continually upward, and their progress can be measured until the flower finally appears at the top of the tall plant. If planted along the wall of a two-story house, beneath an upstairs window, the progress can be observed from above as well as below, and the flowers will be easier to see.

*T*here are so many sunflower options, and I have never seen one I didn't like.

Birds will flock to the ripening seedheads of your sunflowers, quickly plucking out the tightly packed seeds.

Tips

The lower-growing varieties can be used in beds and borders. The tall varieties are effective at the backs of borders and make good screens and temporary hedges. The tallest varieties may need staking.

Recommended

H. annuus (common sunflower) is considered weedy, but many attractive cultivars have been developed.

Features: late-summer flowers, most commonly yellow, but also orange, red, brown, cream, bicolored; typically with brown, purple, rusty red centers; edible seeds **Height:** dwarf varieties, 24"; giants up to 15' **Spread:** 12–24"

Sweet Alyssum
Lobularia

Sweet alyssum is excellent for creating soft edges, and it self-seeds, popping up along pathways and between stones late in the season to give summer a sweet sendoff.

Growing

Sweet alyssum prefers **full sun** but tolerates light shade. **Well-drained** soil of **average fertility** is preferred, but poor soil is tolerated. Sweet alyssum may die back a bit during the heat and humidity of summer. Trim it back and water it periodically to encourage new growth and more flowers when the weather cools.

Tips

Sweet alyssum creeps around rock gardens, over rock walls and along the edges of beds. It is an excellent choice for seeding into cracks and crevices of walkways and between patio stones, and once established it readily reseeds. It is also good for filling in spaces between taller plants in borders and mixed containers.

Recommended

L. maritima forms a low, spreading mound of foliage. The entire plant appears to be covered in tiny blossoms when in full flower. Cultivars with flowers in a wide range of colors are available.

L. maritima (above & below)

Leave alyssum plants out all winter. In spring, remove the previous year's growth to expose self-sown seedlings below.

Features: fragrant, pink, purple, yellow, salmon, white flowers **Height:** 3–12"
Spread: 6–24"

Verbena
Verbena

V. bonariensis (above), *V. x hybrida* (below)

Verbenas offer butterflies a banquet. Butterfly visitors include tiger swallowtails, silver-spotted skippers, great spangled fritillaries and painted ladies.

Growing

Verbenas grow best in **full sun**. The soil should be **fertile** and very **well drained**. Pinch back young plants for bushy growth.

Tips

Use verbenas on rock walls and in beds, borders, rock gardens, containers, hanging baskets and window boxes. They make good substitutes for ivy-leaved geranium where the sun is hot and where a roof overhang keeps the mildew-prone verbenas dry.

Recommended

V. bonariensis forms a low clump of foliage from which tall, stiff stems bear clusters of small, purple flowers.

V. x hybrida is a bushy plant that may be upright or spreading. It bears clusters of small flowers in a wide range of colors. Cultivars are available.

Also called: garden verbena **Features:** red, pink, purple, blue, yellow, scarlet, silver, peach, white flowers; some with white centers **Height:** 8–60" **Spread:** 12–36"

Aster
Aster

A mong the final plants to bloom before the snow flies, asters often provide a last meal for migrating butterflies. The purples and pinks of asters make a nice contrast to the yellow-flowered perennials common in the late summer garden.

Growing
Asters prefer **full sun** but tolerate partial shade. The soil should be **fertile, moist** and **well drained**. Pinch or shear these plants back in early summer to promote dense growth and reduce disease problems. Mulch in winter to protect plants from temperature fluctuations.

Divide asters every two or three years to maintain vigor and control spread.

Tips
Use asters in the middle of borders and in cottage gardens, or naturalize them in wild gardens.

Recommended
Some aster species have recently been reclassified under the genus *Symphyotrichum*. You may see both names at garden centers.

A. novae-angliae (Michaelmas daisy, New England aster) is an upright, spreading, clump-forming perennial that bears yellow-centered, purple flowers. Many cultivars are available.

A. novi-belgii (Michaelmas daisy, New York aster) is a dense, upright, clumpforming perennial with purple flowers. Many cultivars are available.

A. novi-belgii cultivar (above), *A. novi-belgii* (below)

What looks like a single flower of an aster or other plant with daisy-like flowers, is actually a cluster of many tiny flowers. Look closely at the center of the flowerhead and you will see all the individual florets.

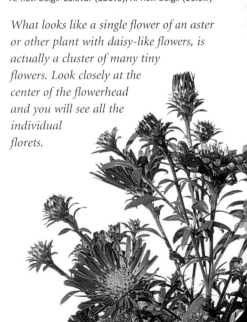

Features: late-summer to mid-autumn flowers in shades of red, white, blue, purple, pink, often with yellow centers **Height:** 10"–5' **Spread:** 18–36" **Hardiness:** zones 3–8

Astilbe
Astilbe

A. x *arendsii* cultivars (above), A. x *arendsii* 'Bressingham Beauty' (below)

Astilbes are beacons in the shade. Their high-impact flowers will brighten any gloomy section of your garden.

Growing

Astilbes grow best in **light or partial shade** but tolerate full shade, though they will not flower as much in full shade. The soil should be **fertile, humus rich, acidic, moist** and **well drained**. Although they appreciate moist soil, astilbes don't like standing water.

Astilbes should be divided every three years or so to maintain plant vigor. Root masses may lift out of the soil as they mature. Add a layer of topsoil and mulch if this occurs.

Tips

Astilbes can be grown near the edges of bog gardens and ponds and in woodland gardens and shaded borders.

Recommended

A. x *arendsii* (astilbe, false spirea, Arend's astilbe) is a group of hybrids with many available cultivars.

A. chinensis (Chinese astilbe) is a dense, vigorous perennial that tolerates dry soil better than other astilbe species. Many cultivars are available.

A. japonica (Japanese astilbe) is a compact, clump-forming perennial. The species is rarely grown in favor of the many cultivars.

Features: attractive foliage; white, pink, purple, peach, red summer flowers
Height: 10"–4' **Spread:** 8–36"
Hardiness: zones 3–9

Bellflower
Campanula

hanks to their wide range of heights and habits, it is possible to put bellflowers almost anywhere in the garden.

Growing

Bellflowers grow well in **full sun, partial shade** or **light shade**. The soil should be of **average to high fertility** and **well drained**. These plants appreciate a mulch to keep their roots cool and moist in summer and protected in winter, particularly if snow cover is inconsistent. Deadhead to prolong blooming.

Tips

Plant upright and mounding bellflowers in borders and cottage gardens. Use low, spreading and trailing bellflowers in rock gardens and on rock walls. You can also edge beds with the low-growing varieties.

Recommended

C. x **'Birch Hybrid'** is a low-growing and spreading plant. It bears light blue to mauve flowers in summer.

C. carpatica (Carpathian bellflower, Carpathian harebell) is a spreading, mounding perennial that bears blue, white or purple flowers in summer. Several cultivars are available.

C. glomerata (clustered bellflower) forms a clump of upright stems and bears clusters of purple, blue or white flowers throughout most of summer.

C. persicifolia (above), *C. carpatica* 'White Clips' (below)

C. persicifolia (peach-leaved bellflower) is an upright perennial that bears white, blue or purple flowers from early summer to mid-summer.

C. poscharskyana (Serbian bellflower) is a trailing perennial that likes to wind its way around other plants. It bears light violet-blue flowers in summer and early autumn.

Also called: campanula **Features:** blue, white, purple or pink spring, summer or autumn flowers; varied growing habits
Height: 4"–6' **Spread:** 12–36"
Hardiness: zones 3–7

Blazing Star
Liatris

L. spicata 'Kobold' (above), L. spicata (below)

The spikes make excellent, long-lasting cut flowers.

Blazing star is an outstanding cut flower with fuzzy, spiked blossoms above grass-like foliage. It is also an excellent plant for attracting butterflies to the garden.

Growing

Blazing star prefers **full sun**. The soil should be of **average fertility, sandy** and **humus rich**. Water well during the growing season, but don't allow the plants to stand in water during cool weather. Mulch during summer to prevent moisture loss.

Trim off the spent flower spikes to promote a longer blooming period and to keep blazing star looking tidy. Divide every three or four years in autumn. The clump will appear crowded when it is time to divide.

Tips

Use this plant in borders and meadow plantings. Plant in a location that has good drainage to avoid root rot in winter. Blazing star grows well in planters.

Recommended

L. spicata is a clump-forming, erect plant. The flowers are pinkish purple or white. Several cultivars are available.

Also called: spike gayfeather, gayfeather
Features: purple or white summer flowers; grass-like foliage **Height:** 18–36"
Spread: 18–24" **Hardiness:** zones 3–9

Bleeding Heart
Dicentra

Every garden should have a bleeding heart plant. Tucked away in a shady spot, this lovely plant appears in spring and fills the garden with fresh promise.

Growing
Bleeding hearts prefer **light shade** but tolerate partial or full shade. The soil should be **humus rich, moist** and **well drained**. Very dry summer conditions cause the plants to die back, though they will revive in autumn or the following spring. Bleeding hearts must remain moist while blooming in order to prolong the flowering period. Regular watering will keep the flowers coming until mid-summer.

Tips
Bleeding hearts can be naturalized in a woodland garden or grown in a border or rock garden. They make excellent early-season specimen plants and do well near ponds or streams.

Recommended
D. eximia (fringed bleeding heart) forms a loose, mounded clump of lacy, fern-like foliage and bears pink or white flowers in spring and sporadically over summer.

D. formosa (western bleeding heart) is a low-growing, wide-spreading plant with pink flowers that fade to white as they mature. The most drought tolerant of the bleeding hearts, it is the most likely to continue flowering all summer.

D. spectabilis (common bleeding heart, Japanese bleeding heart) forms a large, elegant mound that bears flowers with white inner petals and pink outer petals. Several cultivars are available.

D. formosa (above), *D. spectabilis* (below)

All bleeding hearts contain toxic alkaloids, and some people develop allergic skin reactions from contact with these plants.

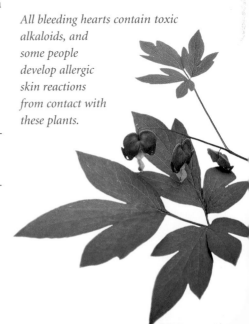

Features: pink, white, red or purple spring and summer flowers; attractive foliage **Height:** 1–4'
Spread: 12–36" **Hardiness:** zones 3–9

Bugbane
Actaea (Cimicifuga)

A. racemosa (above & below)

A. racemosa *is also known as black cohosh, and the rhizomes are used in herbal medicine.*

Bugbanes put on impressive displays. These tall plants bear fragrant flowers above decorative foliage.

Growing
Bugbanes grow best in **partial or light shade**. The soil should be **fertile, humus rich** and **moist**. The plants may require support from a peony hoop.

The plants spread by rhizomes; small pieces of root can be carefully unearthed and replanted in spring if more plants are desired.

Tips
Bugbanes make attractive additions to an open woodland garden, shaded border or pondside planting. They don't compete well with tree roots or other plants that have vigorous roots. Bugbanes are worth growing close to the house because the late-season flowers are wonderfully fragrant.

Recommended
A. racemosa (black snakeroot) is a clump-forming perennial with long-stemmed spikes of fragrant, creamy white flowers.

A. simplex (Kamchatka bugbane) is a clump-forming perennial with fragrant bottlebrush-like spikes of flowers. Several cultivars are available, including those with bronze or purple foliage.

Also called: snakeroot **Features:** fragrant, white, cream or pink late-summer and autumn flowers, some with bronze or purple foliage **Height:** 3–8' **Spread:** 24" **Hardiness:** zones 3–8

Chrysanthemum
Chrysanthemum

Perk up your fall garden with a bright display of fall mums, with their masses of colorful flowers.

Growing
Chrysanthemums grow best in **full sun**. The soil should be **fertile, moist** and **well drained**. Plant as early in the growing season as possible to increase the chances that chrysanthemums will survive the winter. Pinch plants back in early summer to encourage bushy growth and to increase flower production. Divide plants every two or three years to keep them growing vigorously.

Tips
Chrysanthemums provide a blaze of color in the fall garden that lasts right until the first hard frost. In groups or as specimen plants, they can be included in borders, in planters or in plantings close to the house. If they are purchased in fall, they can be added to spots where summer annuals have faded.

Recommended
C. Hybrids form a diverse group of plant series with varied hardiness in Pennsylvania. A few popular hybrids are **C. 'Mei-Kyo,'** a vigorous grower that produces deep pink flowers in mid- to late October, and **C. 'Prophet'** has cultivars with flowers in a wide range of colors, including **'Christine'** with deep salmon pink flowers and **'Raquel'** with bright red flowers.

C. hybrids (above & below)

Although the genus name Chrysanthemum *comes from the Greek and means 'golden flower,' these plants actually bloom in a wide range of bright colors.*

Features: late-summer or fall flowers in shades of orange, red, yellow, pink, red, purple; habit
Height: 12–36" **Spread:** 2–4'
Hardiness: zones 5–9

Columbine
Aquilegia

A. x *hybrida* 'McKana Hybrids' (above & below)

Delicate and beautiful columbines add a touch of simple elegance to any garden. Blooming from the cool of spring through to mid-summer, these long-lasting flowers herald the passing of spring and the arrival of warm summer weather.

Growing
Columbines grow well in **light or partial shade**. They prefer soil that is **fertile, moist** and **well drained**, but they adapt to most soil conditions. Division is not required but can be done to propagate desirable plants. The divided plants may take a

while to recover because columbines dislike having their roots disturbed.

Tips
Use columbines in rock gardens, formal or casual borders and naturalized or woodland gardens.

Recommended
A. canadensis (wild columbine, Canada columbine) is a native plant that is common in woodlands and fields. It bears yellow flowers with red spurs.

A. x *hybrida* (*A.* x *cultorum*; hybrid columbine) forms mounds of delicate foliage and has exceptional flowers. Many hybrids have been developed with showy flowers in a wide range of colors.

A. vulgaris (European columbine, common columbine) has been used to develop many hybrids and cultivars with flowers in a variety of colors.

Features: red, yellow, pink, purple, blue or white spring and summer flowers; color of spurs often differs from that of the petals; attractive foliage **Height:** 18–36"
Spread: 12–24" **Hardiness:** zones 3–9

Daylily
Hemerocallis

The daylily's adaptability and durability combined with its variety in color, blooming period, size and texture explain this perennial's popularity.

Growing
Daylilies grow in any light from **full sun to full shade**. The deeper the shade, the fewer flowers will be produced. The soil should be **fertile, moist** and **well drained**, but these plants adapt to most conditions and are hard to kill once established. Divide them every two or three years to keep the plants vigorous and to propagate them. They can, however, be left indefinitely without dividing.

Tips
Plant daylilies alone, or group them in borders, on banks and in ditches to control erosion. They can be naturalized in woodland or meadow gardens. Small varieties are nice in planters.

'Stella de Oro' (above), 'Bonanza' (below)

Recommended
Daylilies come in an almost infinite number of forms, sizes and colors in a range of species, cultivars and hybrids. Contact your local garden center or daylily grower to find out what's available.

H. citrina (citron daylily) is a Chinese species daylily that is sterile and therefore self-cleaning (no deadheading!). It is hardy from zones 3–8 in full sun to partial shade. A nocturnal bloomer, the extremely fragrant 4–6' scapes of very tight, trumpet-shaped, narrow-petaled, lemon yellow flowers open in the afternoon and bloom through early morning.

(Great for insomniacs and people who have a 9–5 job and usually get to enjoy the garden at night.) Foliage remains unblemished and does not need to be pulled in order to get a fresh flush of growth in late summer.

Features: spring and summer flowers in every color except blue and pure white; grass-like foliage **Height:** 1–4' **Spread:** 1–4' **Hardiness:** zones 2–9

False Indigo
Baptisia

B. australis (above & below)

Spikes of bright blue flowers in early summer and attractive green foliage make this plant a worthy addition even if it does take up a sizable amount of garden real estate.

Growing
False indigo prefers **full sun** but tolerates partial shade. Too much shade causes lank growth that flops over easily. The soil for this native prairie plant should be of **poor to average fertility, sandy** and **well drained**.

Tips
False indigo can be used in an informal border or cottage garden. It is an attractive addition for a naturalized planting, on a slope or in any sunny, well-drained spot in the garden.

Recommended
B. australis is an upright or somewhat spreading, clump-forming plant that bears spikes of purple-blue flowers in early summer.

Also called: baptisia **Features:** purple-blue late-spring or early-summer flowers; habit; foliage **Height:** 3–5' **Spread:** 2–4' **Hardiness:** zones 3–9

Foamflower
Tiarella

Foamflowers form handsome groundcovers in shaded areas, with attractive leaves and delicate, starry white flowers.

Growing

Foamflowers prefer **partial, light or full shade** without afternoon sun. The soil should be **humus rich, moist** and **slightly acidic**. These plants adapt to most soils. Divide in spring. Deadhead to encourage reblooming. If the foliage fades or develops rust in summer, cut it partway to the ground; new growth will emerge.

Tips

Foamflowers are excellent groundcovers for shaded and woodland gardens. They can be included in shaded borders and left to naturalize in wild gardens.

Recommended

T. cordifolia is a low-growing, spreading plant that bears spikes of foamy-looking, white flowers. Cultivars are available.

T. 'Maple Leaf' is a clump-forming hybrid with bronze-green, maple-like leaves and pink-flushed flowers.

T. cordifolia 'Pink Bouquet' (above), T. cordifolia (below)

These plants spread by underground stems, which are easily pulled up to stop excessive spread.

Features: white or pink spring and sometimes early-summer flowers; decorative foliage
Height: 4–12" **Spread:** 12–24"
Hardiness: zones 3–8

Goat's Beard
Aruncus

A. dioicus (above & below)

Male and female flowers are produced on separate plants. In general, male flowers are full and fuzzy while female flowers are more pendulous, though it can be difficult to tell the two apart.

Despite its imposing size, goat's beard has a soft and delicate appearance with its divided foliage and large, plumy, cream-colored flowers.

Growing
These plants prefer **partial to full shade**. If planted in deep shade, they bear fewer blooms. They tolerate some sun as long as the soil is kept evenly moist and they are protected from the afternoon sun. The soil should be **fertile, moist** and **humus rich**.

Tips
These plants look very natural growing near the sunny entrance or edge of a woodland garden, in a native plant garden or in a large island planting. They may also be used in a border or alongside a stream or pond.

Recommended
A. aethusifolius (dwarf Korean goat's beard) forms a low-growing, compact mound and bears branched spikes of loosely held, cream flowers.

A. dioicus (giant goat's beard, common goat's beard) forms a large, bushy, shrub-like perennial with large plumes of creamy white flowers. There are several cultivars.

Features: cream or white, early to mid-summer blooms; shrub-like habit; attractive foliage and seedheads **Height:** 6"–6'
Spread: 1–6' **Hardiness:** zones 3–7

Hardy Geranium

Geranium

*T*here is a type of geranium that suits every garden, thanks to the beauty and diversity of this hardy plant.

Growing

Hardy geraniums grow well in **full sun, partial shade** or **light shade**. These plants dislike hot weather and prefer soil of **average fertility** and **good drainage**. *G. renardii* prefers a poor, well-drained soil. Divide in spring.

Tips

These long-flowering plants are great in a border; they fill in the spaces between shrubs and other larger plants and keep the weeds down. They can be included in rock gardens and woodland gardens, or mass planted as groundcovers.

Recommended

G. **'Brookside'** is a clump-forming, drought-tolerant geranium with finely cut leaves and deep blue to violet-blue flowers.

G. macrorrhizum (bigroot geranium, scented cranesbill) forms a spreading mound of fragrant foliage and bears flowers in various shades of pink. Cultivars are available.

G. renardii (Renard's geranium) forms a clump of velvety, deeply veined, crinkled foliage. A few purple-veined, white flowers appear over summer, but the foliage remains the main attraction.

G. sanguineum (bloodred cranesbill, bloody cranesbill) forms a dense, mounding clump and bears bright magenta flowers. Many cultivars are available.

G. sanguineum var. *striatum* (above)
G. sanguineum (below)

If the foliage looks tatty in late summer, prune it back to rejuvenate it.

Also called: cranesbill geranium **Features:** white, red, pink, purple, blue summer flowers; attractive, sometimes fragrant foliage **Height:** 4–36" **Spread:** 12–36" **Hardiness:** zones 3–8

Hellebore

Helleborus

H. orientalis (above)

This perennial, with its attractive, cup-shaped flowers of green, cream, maroon, pink, yellow or white, may begin flowering as early as February.

Growing

Hellebores prefer **light, dappled shade** and a **sheltered location** but tolerate some direct sun if the soil stays evenly moist. The soil should be **fertile, humus rich, neutral to alkaline, moist** and **well**

drained. Mulch plants in winter if they are planted in an exposed location. Cut off the previous year's foliage when the new flower buds appear.

Tips

Use these plants in a sheltered border or rock garden, or naturalize in a woodland garden. Hellebores are deer resistant.

Recommended

H. foetidus is an upright plant with very attractive, finely dissected foliage that smells unpleasant when crushed. It bears clusters of green, sometimes fragrant, flowers from midwinter to spring. It grows up to 32" tall. (Zones 6–9)

H. x *hybridus* plants grow to about 18" tall, may be deciduous or evergreen, and bloom in a wide range of colors. Cultivars can have single or double flowers in light or deep shades and can be spotted, picoteed or ruffled. (Zones 5–9)

H. niger (Christmas rose) and *H. orientalis* (Lenten rose) form clumps of evergreen foliage. Christmas rose grows to about 12" tall and bears more upward-facing flowers in late winter or early spring. Lenten rose grows 12–24" tall and flowers in mid- to late spring. The flowers of both are white or greenish white and they turn pink as they age.

All parts of hellebores are toxic, and the leaf edges can be quite sharp, so wear long sleeves and gloves when handling or dividing these plants.

Features: white, green, pink, purple, yellow winter to spring flowers; evergreen foliage
Height: 12–32" **Spread:** 18"
Hardiness: zones 4–9

Heuchera
Heuchera

From soft yellow-greens and oranges to midnight purples and silvery, dappled maroons, heucheras offer a great variety of foliage options for a perennial garden with partial shade.

Growing

Heucheras grow best in **light or partial shade**. The foliage colors can bleach out in full sun, and plants grow leggy in full shade. The soil should be of **average to rich fertility, humus rich, neutral to alkaline, moist** and **well drained**. Good air circulation is essential. Deadhead to prolong the bloom.

Every two or three years, heucheras should be dug up and the oldest, woodiest roots and stems removed. Plants may be divided at this time, if desired, then replanted with the crown at or just above soil level.

Tips

Use heucheras as edging plants, in clusters and woodland gardens or as groundcovers in low-traffic areas. Combine different foliage types for an interesting display.

Recommended

There are dozens of beautiful cultivars available with almost limitless variations of foliage markings and colors. Visit your local garden center or view a mail-order catalog to see what is available.

H. x. brizoides 'Firefly' (above), *H. sanguinea* (below)

Heucheras have a strange habit of pushing themselves up out of the soil because of their shallow root systems. Mulch in autumn if the plants begin heaving from the ground.

Also called: coral bells, alum root
Features: very decorative foliage; red, pink, white, yellow, purple spring or summer flowers
Height: 1–4' **Spread:** 6–18"
Hardiness: zones 3–9

Hosta
Hosta

H. *sieboldiana* 'Elegans' (above)

Breeders are always looking for new variations in hosta foliage. Swirls, stripes, puckers and ribs enhance the leaves' various sizes, shapes and colors.

Growing

Hostas prefer **light or partial shade** but will grow in full shade. Morning sun is preferable to afternoon sun in partial shade situations. The soil should ideally be **fertile, moist** and **well drained** but most soils are tolerated. Hostas are fairly drought tolerant, especially if given a mulch to help retain moisture.

Division is not required but can be done every few years in spring or summer to propagate new plants.

Tips

Hostas make wonderful woodland plants and look very attractive when combined with ferns and other fine-textured plants. Hostas are also good plants for a mixed border, particularly when used to hide the ugly, leggy, lower stems and branches of some shrubs. Hostas' dense growth and thick, shade-providing leaves allow them to suppress weeds.

Recommended

Hostas have been subjected to a great deal of crossbreeding and hybridizing, resulting in hundreds of cultivars. Contact your local garden center or get a mail-order catalog to find out what's available.

Some gardeners think the flowers clash with the foliage, and they remove the flower stems when they first emerge. If you find the flowers unattractive, removing them won't harm the plant.

Also called: plantain lily **Features:** decorative foliage; white or purple summer and autumn flowers **Height:** 4–36" **Spread:** 6"–6' **Hardiness:** zones 3–8

Iris

Iris

*I*rises are steeped in history and lore. Many say the range in flower colors of bearded irises approximates that of a rainbow.

Growing

Irises prefer **full sun** but tolerate very light or dappled shade. The soil should be of **average fertility** and **well drained**. Japanese iris and Siberian iris prefer a moist but still well-drained soil. Divide in late summer or early autumn. Deadhead irises to keep them tidy. Cut back the foliage of Siberian iris in spring.

Tips

All irises are popular border plants, but Japanese iris and Siberian iris are also useful alongside streams or ponds. Dwarf cultivars make attractive additions to rock gardens.

Recommended

There are many iris species and hybrids available. Among the most popular is the bearded iris, often a hybrid of **I. germanica**. It has the widest range of flower colors but is susceptible to attack from the iris borer, which can kill a plant. Several irises are not susceptible, including Japanese iris (**I. ensata**) and Siberian iris (**I. sibirica**). Check with your local garden center to find out what's available.

I. sibirica (above), *I. germanica* 'Stepping Out' (below)

Irises can cause severe stomach irritation if ingested, so wash your hands after handling them.

Features: spring, summer and sometimes autumn flowers in many shades of pink, red, purple, blue, white, brown, yellow; attractive foliage **Height:** 4"–4' **Spread:** 6"–4' **Hardiness:** zones 3–10

Lady's Mantle
Alchemilla

A. *mollis* (above & below)

$\mathcal{F}$ew other perennials look as captivating as lady's mantle when droplets of morning dew cling like shimmering pearls to its velvety leaves.

Growing
Lady's mantle grows well in **light shade** or **partial shade** with protection from the afternoon sun. Hot locations and excessive sun will scorch the leaves. The soil should be **fertile, humus rich, moist** and **well drained**.

The leaves can be sheared back in summer if they begin to look tired and heat stressed. New leaves will emerge. Spent flowers can be removed to reduce self-seeding.

Tips
Lady's mantle is ideal for grouping under trees in the dappled shade of a woodland garden and along border and pathway edges, where it softens the bright colors of other plants. It also looks attractive in containers. Compact selections are well suited to rock gardens.

Recommended
A. mollis (common lady's mantle) forms a mound of soft, rounded foliage and produces sprays of frothy-looking, yellowish green flowers in early summer. It grows 8–18" tall and spreads about 24".

Features: yellow or yellow-green summer and early-fall flowers; attractive foliage; habit
Height: 3–18" **Spread:** 20–24"
Hardiness: zones 3–7

Lavender
Lavandula

L avender is considered the queen of herbs. With both the aromatic and ornamental qualities, it makes a valuable addition to any garden.

Growing

Lavenders grow best in **full sun**. The soil should be **average to fertile** and **alkaline**, and it must be **well drained**. Once established, these plants are heat and drought tolerant. Protect plants from winter cold and wind. In colder areas, lavenders should receive additional mulching and, with luck, a good layer of snow. Plants can be sheared in spring or after flowering.

Tips

Lavenders are wonderful, aromatic edging plants. They can be planted in drifts or as specimens in small spaces, or used to form a low hedge.

Recommended

L. angustifolia (English lavender) is an aromatic, bushy subshrub. It grows to about 24" tall with an equal spread. From mid-summer to fall, it bears spikes of small, light purple flowers. Many cultivars are available, including selections with white or pink flowers, silvery gray to olive green foliage and dwarf or compact habits.

L. x *intermedia* (lavandin) is a natural hybrid between English lavender and spike lavender (*L. latifolia*). It grows 36" tall with an equal spread. The flowers are held on long spikes. Cultivars are available.

Features: purple, pink, blue, white mid-summer to fall flowers; fragrance; evergreen foliage; habit **Height:** 8–36" **Spread:** up to 4' **Hardiness:** zones 5–9

L. angustifolia (above & below)

The sensuous scent of lavender is relaxing and soothing, and is used in aromatherapy, lavender sachets and potpourri.

Meadow Rue
Thalictrum

T. rochebruneanum 'Lavender Mist' (above), *T. aquilegifolium* (below)

Meadow rues are tall without being overbearing. Their fluffy flowers sway gracefully in the wind on wiry stems above fine foliage.

Growing
Meadow rues prefer **light or partial shade** but tolerate full sun with moist soil. The soil should be **humus rich, moist** and **well drained.** Meadow rues dislike being disturbed, and plants may take a while to re-establish once they have been divided.

Tips
Meadow rues look beautiful when naturalized in an open woodland or meadow

garden. In the middle or at the back of a border, they make a soft backdrop for bolder plants and flowers.

These plants often do not emerge until quite late in spring. Mark where you plant them so that you do not inadvertently disturb the roots while cultivating their bed before they begin to grow.

Recommended
T. aquilegifolium (columbine meadow rue) forms an upright mound with pink or white plumes of flowers. Cultivars are available.

T. rochebruneanum **'Lavender Mist'** (lavender mist meadow rue) forms a narrow, upright clump. The blooms are lavender purple and have numerous, distinctive yellow stamens.

Features: pink, purple, yellow, white summer flowers; light, airy habit; attractive foliage
Height: 2–5' **Spread:** 12–36"
Hardiness: zones 3–8

Meadowsweet

Filipendula

For an impressive, informal, vertical accent and showy clusters of fluffy, fragrant flowers, meadowsweets are second to none.

Growing

Meadowsweets prefer **partial or light shade** but tolerate full sun if the soil remains sufficiently moist. The soil should be **fertile, deep, humus rich** and **moist**, except in the case of *F. vulgaris*, which prefers dry soil. Divide in spring or autumn.

Tips

Most meadowsweets are excellent plants for bog gardens or wet sites. Plant them alongside streams or in moist meadows. Meadowsweets may also be grown in the back of a border, as long as they are kept well watered. Grow *F. vulgaris* if you can't provide the moisture needed by the other species.

Recommended

F. rubra (queen-of-the-prairie) forms a large, spreading clump and bears clusters of fragrant, pink flowers. Cultivars are available.

F. ulmaria (queen-of-the-meadow) forms a mounding clump and bears creamy white flowers in large clusters. Cultivars are available.

F. vulgaris (dropwort, meadowsweet) is a low-growing species that bears clusters of fragrant, creamy white flowers. Cultivars with double or pink flowers or variegated foliage are available.

F. ulmaria 'Variegata (above), F. ulmaria (below)

Deadhead meadowsweets if you so desire, but the faded seedheads are quite attractive when left in place.

Features: white, cream, pink, red late spring or summer flowers; attractive foliage **Height:** 2–8' **Spread:** $1^1/_2$–4' **Hardiness:** zones 3–8

Peony

Paeonia

P. *lactiflora* 'Shimmering Velvet' (above)
P. *lactiflora* cultivars (below)

From the simple, single flowers to the extravagant doubles, it's easy to become mesmerized with these voluptuous plants. Once the fleeting, but magnificent, flower display is done, the foliage remains stellar throughout the growing season.

Growing

Peonies prefer **full sun** but tolerate some shade. The planting site should be well prepared before the plants are introduced.

Peonies prefer **fertile, humus-rich, moist, well-drained** soil to which a lot of compost has been added. Mulch peonies lightly with compost in spring. Too much fertilizer, particularly nitrogen, causes floppy growth and retards blooming. Division is not required but can be done in autumn to propagate plants. Deadhead to keep plants looking tidy.

Tips

These wonderful plants look great in a border combined with other early bloomers. They may be underplanted with bulbs and other plants that will die down by mid-summer—the emerging foliage of peonies will hide the dying foliage of spring plants. Avoid planting peonies under trees where they will have to compete for moisture and nutrients.

Planting depth determines whether a peony will flower. Tubers planted too shallow or, more commonly, too deep, will not flower. The buds or eyes on the tuber should be 1–2" below the soil surface.

Place peony cages around the plants in early spring to support the heavy flowers. The foliage will grow up into the wires and hide the cage.

Recommended

There are hundreds of peonies available. Cultivars come in a wide range of colors, may have single or double flowers, and may or may not be fragrant. Visit your local garden center to see what is available.

Features: white, cream white, yellow, pink, red, purple spring and early-summer flowers; attractive foliage **Height:** 24–32" **Spread:** 24–32" **Hardiness:** zones 2–7

Pinks
Dianthus

D. deltoides (above), *D. plumarius* (below)

From tiny and delicate to large and robust, this genus contains a wide variety of plants, many with spice-scented flowers.

Growing

Pinks prefer **full sun** but tolerate some shade. A **well-drained, neutral or alkaline** soil is required. The most important factor in the successful cultivation of pinks is drainage—they hate to stand in water. Rocky outcroppings make up the native habitat of many species.

Tips

Pinks make excellent plants for rock gardens and rock walls, and for edging flower borders and walkways. They can also be used in cutting gardens and even as groundcovers. To prolong blooming, deadhead as the flowers fade, but leave a few flowers in place to go to seed.

Recommended

D. x *allwoodii* (allwood pink) is a hybrid that forms a compact mound and bears flowers in a wide range of colors. Many cultivars are available.

D. *deltoides* (maiden pink) forms a mat of foliage and flowers in shades of red.

D. *gratianopolitanus* (cheddar pink) is long-lived and forms a very dense mat of evergreen, silver gray foliage with sweet-scented flowers mostly in shades of pink.

D. *plumarius* (cottage pink) is noteworthy for its role in the development of many popular cultivars known collectively as garden pinks. The flowers can be single, semi-double or fully double and are available in many colors.

Features: sometimes-fragrant pink, red, white, purple spring or summer flowers; attractive foliage **Height:** 2–18" **Spread:** 6–24" **Hardiness:** zones 3–9

Plume Poppy
Macleaya

M. cordata (above & below)

Deadhead if you do not want self-sown seedlings popping up all over.

Plume poppy is bold, not only in its visual presence, but also in its space-grabbing maneuvers.

Growing
Plume poppy prefers **full sun** but tolerates partial shade. The soil should be of **average fertility, humus rich** and **moist**. Plume poppy tolerates dry soils and is less invasive in poorer conditions. Divide every two or three years in spring or autumn to control the size of the clump.

Pull up or cut back any overly exuberant growth as needed. Planting in a heavy-duty, bottomless pot sunk into the ground will slow invasive spreading.

Tips
Plume poppy makes an impressive specimen plant and looks good at the back of a border. It quickly creates a summer screen and makes a good choice for the center of a cement-bordered median or large island bed.

Recommended
M. cordata is a tall, narrow, clump-forming plant with attractive, undulating, lobed leaves and plumes of creamy white flowers.

Features: cream-colored, mid- to late-summer flowers; attractive foliage; shrub-like plants
Height: 6–10' **Spread:** 12–36"; clumps can spread indefinitely **Hardiness:** zones 3–10

Purple Coneflower

Echinacea

Purple coneflower is a visual delight, with its mauve petals offset by a spiky, orange center.

Growing

Purple coneflower grows well in **full sun** or very **light shade**. It tolerates any **well-drained** soil but prefers an **average to rich** soil. The thick tap-roots make this plant drought resistant, but it prefers to have regular water. Divide every four years or so in spring or fall.

Deadhead early in the flowering season to prolong blooming. Later you may wish to leave the flowerheads in place to self-seed and provide winter interest. Pinch plants back or thin out the stems in early summer to encourage bushy growth that is less prone to mildew.

Tips

Use purple coneflowers in meadow gardens and informal borders, either in groups or as single specimens.

The dry flowerheads make an interesting feature in autumn and winter gardens.

Recommended

E. purpurea is an upright plant covered in prickly hairs. It bears purple flowers with orangy centers. Cultivars are available.

E. purpurea (above & below)

Purple coneflower attracts wildlife to the garden, providing pollen, nectar and seeds to a variety of hungry visitors.

Also called: coneflower, echinacea **Features:** purple, pink, white mid-summer to autumn flowers with rusty orange centers; persistent seedheads **Height:** 2–5' **Spread:** 12–24" **Hardiness:** zones 3–8

Russian Sage
Perovskia

P. atriplicifolia (above), *P. atriplicifolia* 'Filgran' (below)

Russian sage offers four-season interest in the garden: soft, gray-green leaves on light gray stems in spring; fuzzy, violet-blue flowers in summer; and silvery white stems in autumn that last until late winter.

Growing

Russian sage prefers **full sun**. The soil should be **poor to moderately fertile** and **well drained**. Too much water and nitrogen will cause this plant's

Russian sage blossoms make a lovely addition to fresh bouquets and dried-flower arrangements.

growth to flop, so do not plant it next to heavy feeders. Russian sage cannot be divided because it is a subshrub that originates from a single stem.

In spring, when new growth appears low on the branches, or in autumn, cut the plant back hard to about 6–12" to encourage vigorous, bushy growth.

Tips

The silvery foliage and blue flowers work well with other plants in the back of a mixed border and soften the appearance of daylilies. Russian sage can also create a soft screen in a natural garden or on a dry bank.

Recommended

P. atriplicifolia is a loose, upright plant with silvery white, finely divided foliage. The small, lavender blue flowers are loosely held on silvery, branched stems. Cultivars are available.

Features: blue or purple mid-summer to autumn flowers; attractive habit; fragrant gray-green foliage **Height:** 3–4' **Spread:** 3–4' **Hardiness:** zones 4–9

Sedum

Sedum

Some 300 to 500 species of sedum are distributed throughout the Northern Hemisphere. Many sedums are grown for their foliage, which can range in color from steel gray-blue and green to red and burgundy.

Growing

Sedums prefer **full sun** but tolerate partial shade. The soil should be of **average fertility,** very **well drained** and **neutral to alkaline**. Divide in spring when needed.

Tips

Low-growing sedums make wonderful groundcovers and additions to rock gardens or rock walls. They also edge beds and borders beautifully. Taller sedums give a lovely late-season display in a bed or border.

Recommended

S. acre (gold moss stonecrop) is a low-growing, wide-spreading plant that bears small, yellow-green flowers.

S. 'Autumn Joy' (autumn joy sedum) is a popular, upright hybrid. The flowers open pink or red and later fade to deep bronze.

S. spectabile (showy stonecrop) is an upright species with pink flowers. Cultivars are available.

S. spurium (two-row stonecrop) forms a low, wide mat of foliage with deep pink or white flowers. Many cultivars are available and are often grown for their colorful foliage.

S. 'Autumn Joy' (above & below)

Early-summer pruning of upright species and hybrids encourages compact, bushy growth but can delay flowering.

Also called: stonecrop **Features:** yellow, white, red, pink summer to autumn flowers; decorative, fleshy foliage **Height:** 2–24"
Spread: 12–24" or more
Hardiness: zones 3–8

Stokes' Aster

Stokesia

S. laevis (above & below)

Stokes' aster is an easy, adaptable, late-summer blooming perennial that flowers in a wide range of colors. Foliage stays green throughout winter.

Growing
Stokes' aster grows and blooms best in **full sun**. The soil should be **fertile to average, light, acidic, moist** and **well drained**. The soil should be on the dry side while plants are dormant in winter. Deadhead as soon as flowers begin to fade to encourage blooming. Divide in late winter or spring. Stokes' aster self-sows, but not invasively.

Tips
Stokes' aster is a favorite of butterflies and will attract these and other pollinators to your garden. Include this plant in mixed and perennial beds and borders. The flowers are long-lasting in fresh flower arrangements.

Recommended
S. laevis is a sturdy, upright, evergreen perennial with woolly, squarish stems. It grows 24" tall. There are many cultivars available. **'Alba'** has white flowers. **'Blue Danube'** and **'Peachie's Pick'** have long-lasting blue flowers. COLORWHEEL bears flowers that open white and mature to dark purple. Many flowers are open at once, creating an impressive display of varied shades. **'Klaus Jelitto'** has exceptionally large, blue flowers. **'Mary Gregory'** has pale yellow flowers. **'Omega Skyrocket'** bears pale blue flowers on stems 3–4' high. **'Purple Parasols'** has deep violet blossoms. **'Rosea'** has deep pink, powderpuff blooms.

Features: white, pink, blue, purple, yellow summer to fall flowers; evergreen foliage
Height: 12–24" **Spread:** 18–24"
Hardiness: zones 5–10

Yarrow
Achillea

*Y*arrows are informal, tough plants with a fantastic color range.

Growing

Yarrows grow best in **full sun**. The soil should be of **average fertility, sandy** and **well drained**. These plants tolerate drought and poor soil. They also tolerate heavy, wet soil and humidity, but they do not thrive in such conditions. Excessively rich soil or too much nitrogen results in weak, floppy growth. Divide every two or three years in spring.

Deadhead to prolong blooming. Basal foliage should be left in place over the winter and tidied up in spring.

Tips

Cottage gardens, wildflower gardens and mixed borders are perfect places for these informal plants. They thrive in hot, dry locations where nothing else will grow.

Recommended

A. filipendulina forms a clump of ferny foliage and bears yellow flowers. It has been used to develop several hybrids and cultivars.

A. millefolium (common yarrow) forms a clump of soft, finely divided foliage and bears white flowers. Many cultivars exist, with flowers in a wide range of colors.

Features: white, yellow, red, orange, pink, purple mid-summer to early-autumn flowers; attractive foliage; spreading habit
Height: 4"–4' **Spread:** 12–36"
Hardiness: zones 3–9

A. *millefolium* 'Paprika' (above)
A. *filipendulina* hybrid (below)

Yarrows make excellent groundcovers. They send up shoots and flowers from a low basal point and may be mowed periodically without excessive damage to the plant. Mower blades should be kept at least 4" high.

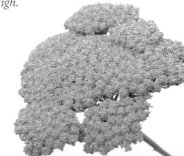

Beech

Fagus

F. sylvatica 'Pendula' (above), *F. sylvatica* (below)

The aristocrats of the large shade trees, the majestic beeches are attractive at any age, from their big, bold, beautiful youth through to their slow, craggy decline.

Growing

Beeches grow equally well in **full sun** or **partial shade**. The soil should be of **average fertility, loamy** and **well drained**, though almost all well-drained soils are tolerated.

American beech doesn't like having its roots disturbed and should be transplanted only when very young. European beech transplants easily and is more tolerant of varied soil conditions than is American beech.

Tips

Beeches make excellent specimens. They are also used as shade trees and in woodland gardens. These trees need a lot of space, but the European beech's adaptability to pruning makes it a reasonable choice in a small garden if you are willing and able to prune it.

Recommended

F. grandifolia (American beech) is a broad-canopied tree native to most of eastern North America.

F. sylvatica (European beech) is a spectacular, broad tree with a number of interesting cultivars. Several are small enough to use in the home garden, from narrow columnar and weeping varieties to varieties with purple or yellow leaves or pink, white and green variegated foliage.

Features: large, oval, deciduous shade tree; foliage; bark; habit; fall color; fruit
Height: 30–80' **Spread:** 10–65'
Hardiness: zones 4–9

Caryopteris
Caryopteris

Caryopteris is cultivated for its aromatic stems, foliage and flowers. A few cut stems in a vase will delicately scent a room.

Growing

Caryopteris prefers **full sun** but tolerates light shade. It does best in soil of **average fertility** that is **light** and **well drained**. Wet and poorly drained soils can kill this plant. Caryopteris is very drought tolerant once established. It can be treated as a herbaceous perennial if growth is regularly killed back over the winter.

Tips

Include caryopteris in your shrub or mixed border. The bright blue, late-season flowers are welcome when many other plants are past their flowering best.

Recommended

C. x *clandonensis* forms a dense mound that grows up to 36" tall and 3–5' in spread. It bears clusters of blue or purple flowers in late summer and early fall. Cultivars are available and are more often grown than the species.

C. x *clandonensis* 'Dark Knight' (above)
C. x *clandonensis* (below)

Caryopteris is sometimes killed back over cold winters. Cut back the dead growth in spring. New shoots will sprout from the base, providing plenty of late-summer flowers.

Also called: bluebeard, blue spirea
Features: rounded, spreading, deciduous shrub; attractive, fragrant foliage, twigs and late-summer flowers **Height:** 2–4'
Spread: 2–5' **Hardiness:** zones 5–9

Cedar
Thuja

T. occidentalis 'Yellow Ribbon' (above)
T. occidentalis (below)

Cedars are rot resistant, durable and long-lived, earning them quiet admiration from gardeners everywhere.

Growing

Cedars prefer **full sun** but tolerate light to partial shade. The soil should be of **average fertility, moist** and **well drained**. These plants enjoy humidity and in the wild are often found growing near marshy areas. Cedars will perform best in a location with some shelter from wind, especially in winter when the foliage can easily dry out and give the entire plant a rather brown, drab appearance.

Tips

Large varieties of cedar make excellent specimen trees, and smaller cultivars can be used in foundation plantings and shrub borders, and as formal or informal hedges.

Recommended

T. occidentalis (eastern arborvitae, eastern white cedar) is a narrow, pyramidal tree with scale-like, evergreen needles. There are dozens of cultivars available, including shrubby dwarf varieties, varieties with yellow foliage and smaller, upright varieties. (Zones 2–7; cultivars may be less cold hardy)

T. plicata (western arborvitae, western redcedar) is a narrowly pyramidal evergreen tree that grows quickly, resists deer browsing and maintains good foliage color all winter. Several cultivars are available, including several dwarf varieties and a yellow and green variegated variety. (Zones 5–9)

Also called: arborvitae **Features:** small to large evergreen shrub or tree; foliage; bark; form **Height:** 2–50' **Spread:** 2–20' **Hardiness:** zones 2–9

Cotoneaster

Cotoneaster

C. apiculatus (above), *C. dammeri* (below)

$\mathcal{W}$ith their diverse sizes, shapes, flowers, fruit and foliage, cotoneasters are so versatile that they border on being overused.

Growing

Cotoneasters grow well in **full sun** or **partial shade**. The soil should be of **average fertility** and **well drained**.

Tips

Cotoneasters can be included in shrub or mixed borders. Low spreaders work well as groundcover, and shrubby species can be used to form hedges. Larger species are grown as small specimen trees, and some low growers are grafted onto standards and grown as small weeping trees.

Recommended

There are many cotoneasters to choose from. *C. adpressus* (creeping cotoneaster), *C.* x 'Hessei' and *C. horizontalis* (rockspray cotoneaster) are low-growing groundcover plants. *C. apiculatus* (cranberry cotoneaster) and *C. dammeri* (bearberry cotoneaster) are low, widespreading, shrubby plants. *C. salicifolius* (willowleaf cotoneaster) is an upright, shrubby plant that can be trained to form a small tree. These are just a few possibilities; your local garden center can help you find a suitable one for your garden.

Features: evergreen or deciduous groundcover, shrub or small tree; foliage; early-summer flowers; persistent fruit; variety of forms **Height:** 6"–15' **Spread:** 3–12' **Hardiness:** zones 4–9

Crabapple
Malus

ure white through deep pink flowers, heights between 5' and 30' with similar spreads, tolerance of winter's extreme cold and summer's baking heat and yellow through candy apple red fruit often persisting through winter—what more could anyone ask from a tree?

Growing

Crabapples prefer **full sun** but tolerate partial shade. The soil should be of **average to rich fertility, moist** and **well drained**. These trees tolerate damp soil.

One of the best ways to prevent the spread of crabapple pests and diseases is to clean up all the leaves and fruit that fall off the tree. Many pests overwinter in the fruit, leaves or soil at the base of the tree. Clearing away their winter shelter helps keep populations under control.

Tips

Crabapples make excellent specimen plants. Many varieties are quite small, so there is one to suit almost any size of garden. Some forms are even small enough to grow in large containers. Crabapples' flexible, young branches make them good choices for creating espalier specimens along a wall or fence.

Recommended

There are hundreds of crabapples available. When choosing a species, variety or cultivar, one of the most important attributes to look for is disease resistance. Even the most beautiful flowers, fruit or habit will never look good if the plant is ravaged by pests or diseases. Ask for information about new, resistant cultivars at your local nursery or garden center.

Features: rounded, mounded or spreading, small to medium deciduous tree; spring flowers; late-season and winter fruit; fall foliage; habit; bark **Height:** 5–30'
Spread: 6–30' **Hardiness:** zones 4–8

Dogwood
Cornus

Whether your garden is wet, dry, sunny or shaded, there is a dogwood for almost every condition. Stem color, leaf variegation, fall color, growth habit, soil adaptability and hardiness are all positive attributes to be found in the dogwoods.

Growing
Dogwoods grow equally well in **full sun, light shade** or **partial shade**, with a slight preference for light shade. The soil should be of **average to high fertility, high in organic matter, neutral or slightly acidic** and **well drained**.

Tips
Shrub dogwoods can be included in a shrub or mixed border. They look best in groups rather than as single specimens. The tree species make wonderful specimen plants and are small enough to include in most gardens. Use them along the edge of a woodland, in a shrub or mixed border, alongside a house, or near a pond, water feature or patio.

Recommended
C. alba (red-twig dogwood, Tartarian dogwood) and *C. sericea* (*C. stolonifera*; red-osier dogwood) are grown for their bright red stems that provide winter interest. Cultivars are available with stems in varied shades of red, orange and yellow. Fall foliage color can also be attractive. (Zones 2–7)

C. alternifolia (pagoda dogwood) can be grown as a large, multi-stemmed shrub or a small, single-stemmed tree.

C. alba 'Bailhalo' (above), *C. kousa* var. *chinensis* (below)

The branches have an attractive layered appearance. Clusters of small, white flowers appear in early summer. (Zones 3–8)

C. kousa (Kousa dogwood) is grown for its flowers, fruit, fall color and interesting bark. The white-bracted flowers are followed by bright red fruit. The foliage turns red and purple in fall. **Var.** *chinensis* (Chinese dogwood) grows more vigorously and has larger flowers. (Zones 5–9)

Features: deciduous, large shrub or small tree; late-spring to early-summer flowers; fall foliage; stem color; fruit; habit **Height:** 5–30' **Spread:** 5–30' **Hardiness:** zones 2–9

Elder

Sambucus

S. canadensis (above), S. racemosa (below)

Both the flowers and the fruit can be used to make wine. The berries are popular for pies and jelly. The raw berries are marginally edible but not palatable and can cause stomach upset, particularly in children. All other parts of elders are toxic.

*E*lders work well in a naturalized garden. Cultivars are available that will provide light texture in a dark area, dark foliage in a bright area, or variegated yellow foliage and bright stems in brilliant sunshine.

Growing

Elders grow well in **full sun** or **partial shade**. Cultivars and varieties grown for interesting leaf color develop the best color in light or partial shade. The soil should be of **average fertility, moist** and **well drained**. These plants tolerate dry soil once established.

Tips

Elders can be used in a shrub or mixed border, in a natural woodland garden or next to a pond or other water feature. Types with interesting or colorful foliage can be used as specimen plants or focal points in the garden.

Recommended

S. canadensis (American elder/elderberry), *S. nigra* (European elder/elderberry, black elder/elderberry) and *S. racemosa* (European red elder/elderberry) are rounded shrubs with white or pinkish white flowers followed by red or dark purple berries. Cultivars are available with green, yellow, bronze or purple foliage and deeply divided, feathery foliage.

Also called: elderberry **Features:** large, bushy, deciduous shrub; early-summer flowers; fruit; foliage **Height:** 5–20' **Spread:** 5–20' **Hardiness:** zones 3–9

Enkianthus
Enkianthus

E. campanulatus (above & below)

One of the best shrubs for adding stunning fall color to your garden.

Growing
Enkianthus grows well in **full sun, partial shade** or **light shade**. The soil should be **fertile, humus rich, moist, acidic** and **well drained**.

Tips
Enkianthus is a beautiful shrub to include in the understory of a woodland garden and can be used in a mixed border or as a specimen plant. It also makes an excellent companion for rhododendrons and other acid-loving plants.

Recommended
E. campanulatus (red-vein enkianthus) is a large, bushy shrub or small tree that grows 10–15' tall, with an equal spread.

It bears clusters of small, white, red-veined, pendulous, bell-shaped flowers in spring. The foliage turns fantastic shades of yellow, orange and red in fall. (Zones 4–7)

E. perulatus (white enkianthus) is a compact shrub that grows 5–6' tall, with an equal spread. It produces white flowers in mid-spring. The foliage turns bright red in fall. (Zones 5–8)

The layered branching and tufted foliage of enkianthus will add a unique touch to your garden.

Features: bushy deciduous shrub or small tree; spring flowers; fall foliage **Height:** 5–15' **Spread:** 5–15' **Hardiness:** zones 4–8

False Cypress
Chamaecyparis

C. pisifera 'Mops' (above), *C. nootkatensis* 'Pendula' (below)

Conifer shoppers are blessed with a marvelous selection of false cypresses that offer color, size, shape and growth habits not available in most other evergreens.

Growing
False cypresses prefer **full sun**. The soil should be **fertile, moist, neutral to acidic** and **well drained**. Alkaline soils are tolerated. In shaded areas, growth may be sparse.

The oils in the foliage of false cypresses may be irritating to sensitive skin.

Tips
Tree varieties are used as specimen plants and for hedging. The dwarf and slow-growing cultivars are used in borders and rock gardens and as bonsai. False cypress shrubs can be grown near the house or as evergreen specimens in large containers.

Recommended
There are several available species of false cypress and many cultivars. The scaly foliage can be in a drooping or strand form, in fan-like or feathery sprays and may be dark green, bright green or yellow. Plant forms vary too, from mounding or rounded to tall and pyramidal or narrow with pendulous branches. Check with your local garden center or nursery to see what is available.

Features: narrow, pyramidal, evergreen tree or shrub; cultivars vary; foliage; habit; cones
Height: 1½–150' **Spread:** 1½–80'
Hardiness: zones 4–8

Flowering Cherry, Plum & Almond

Prunus

C herries are so beautiful and uplifting after the gray days of winter that few gardeners can resist them.

Growing

These flowering fruit trees prefer **full sun**. The soil should be of **average fertility, moist** and **well drained.** Shallow roots will emerge from the lawn if the tree is not getting sufficient water.

P. sargentii (above)

Tips

Prunus species are beautiful as specimen plants and many are small enough to be included in almost any garden. Small species and cultivars can also be included in borders or grouped to form informal hedges or barriers. Pissard plum and purpleleaf sand cherry can be trained to form formal hedges.

Because of the pest problems that afflict many of the cherries, they can be rather short-lived. Choose resistant species such as Sargent cherry or Higan cherry. If you plant a more susceptible species, such as the Japanese flowering cherry, enjoy it while it thrives but be prepared to replace it.

Recommended

Following are a few popular selections from the many species, hybrids and cultivars available. Check with your local nursery or garden center for other possible selections.

P. cerasifera 'Atropurpurea' (Pissard plum) and *P. x cistena* (purpleleaf sand cherry) are shrubby plants grown for their purple foliage and light pink flowers. *P. sargentii* (Sargent cherry) and *P. serrulata* (Japanese flowering cherry) are rounded or spreading trees grown for their white or light pink flowers as well as often-attractive bark and bright fall color.

Features: upright, rounded, spreading or weeping deciduous tree or shrub; spring to early-summer flowers; fruit; bark; fall foliage
Height: 4–75' **Spread:** 4–50'
Hardiness: zones 4–8

Fothergilla
Fothergilla

F. major (above & below)

Flowers, fragrance, fall color and interesting soft tan to brownish stems give fothergillas year-round appeal.

Growing
Fothergillas grow equally well in **full sun** or **partial shade**. In full sun these plants bear the most flowers and have the best fall color. The soil should be of **average fertility, acidic, humus rich, moist** and **well drained**.

Tips
Fothergillas are attractive and useful in shrub or mixed borders, in woodland gardens and when combined with evergreen groundcover.

Recommended
Cultivars are available for both species.

F. gardenii (dwarf fothergilla) is a bushy shrub that bears fragrant, white flowers. The foliage turns yellow, orange and red in fall.

F. major (large fothergilla) is a larger, rounded shrub that bears fragrant, white flowers. The autumn colors are yellow, orange and scarlet.

The bottlebrush-shaped flowers of fothergillas have a delicate honey scent.

Features: dense, rounded or bushy deciduous shrub; spring flowers; scent; fall foliage
Height: 2–10' **Spread:** 2–10'
Hardiness: zones 4–9

Fringe Tree
Chionanthus

C. virginicus (above & below)

*F*ringe trees adapt to a wide range of growing conditions, are cold hardy and are densely covered in silky white, honey-scented flowers that shimmer in the wind over a long period in spring.

Growing

Fringe trees prefer **full sun**. They do best in soil that is **fertile, acidic, moist** and **well drained** but adapt to most soil conditions. In the wild they are often found growing alongside stream banks.

Tips

Fringe trees work well as specimen plants, as part of a border or beside a water feature. Plants begin flowering at a very early age.

Recommended

C. retusus (Chinese fringe tree) is a rounded, spreading shrub or small tree with deeply furrowed, peeling bark and erect, fragrant, white flower clusters. (Zones 5–8)

C. virginicus (white fringe tree) is a small, spreading tree or large shrub that bears drooping, fragrant, white flowers. (Zones 4–8)

Features: rounded or spreading, deciduous, large shrub or small tree; early-summer flowers; bark; habit **Height:** 10–25'
Spread: 10–25' **Hardiness:** zones 4–9

Hawthorn
Crataegus

C. phaenopyrum (above)
C. laevigata 'Paul's Scarlet' (below)

awthorns are uncommonly beautiful trees, with a generous spring show of beautiful, apple-like blossoms, persistent, glossy, red fruit and often good fall color.

Growing
Hawthorns grow equally well in **full sun** or **partial shade**. They adapt to any **well-drained** soil and tolerate urban conditions.

Tips
Hawthorns can be grown as specimen plants or hedges in urban sites, lakeside gardens and exposed locations. They are popular in areas where vandalism is a problem because very few people wish to grapple with plants bearing stiff, 2" long thorns. As a hedge, hawthorns create an almost impenetrable barrier.

These trees are small enough to include in most gardens. With their long, sharp thorns, however, hawthorns might not be a good selection if there are children about.

Recommended
C. laevigata (*C. oxycantha*; English hawthorn) is a low-branching, rounded tree with zigzag layers of thorny branches. It bears white or pink flowers, followed by red fruit in late summer. Many cultivars are available.

C. phaenopyrum (*C. cordata*; Washington hawthorn) is an oval to rounded, thorny tree that bears white flowers and persistent, shiny red fruit in fall. The glossy green foliage turns red and orange in fall.

Features: rounded, deciduous tree; often with a zigzagged, layered branch pattern; late-spring or early-summer flowers; fruit; foliage; thorny branches **Height:** 15–35' **Spread:** 12–35' **Hardiness:** zones 3–8

Hemlock
Tsuga

T. canadensis 'Jeddeloh' (above), *T. canadensis* (below)

Many people would agree that eastern hemlock is one of the most beautiful, graceful, evergreen trees in the world. The movement, softness and agility of this tree make it easy to place in the landscape.

Growing

Hemlock generally grows well in any light from **full sun to full shade**. The soil should be **humus rich, moist** and **well drained**. Hemlock is drought sensitive and grows best in cool, moist conditions. It is also sensitive to air pollution and suffers salt damage, so keep hemlock away from roadways.

Tips

This elegant tree, with its delicate needles, is one of the most beautiful evergreens to use as a specimen tree.

Hemlock can also be trimmed to form a hedge. The smaller cultivars may be included in a shrub or mixed border. Hemlock can be pruned to keep it within bounds or shaped to form a hedge. The many dwarf forms are useful in smaller gardens.

Recommended

T. canadensis (eastern hemlock, Canadian hemlock) is a graceful, narrowly pyramidal tree. Many cultivars are available, including groundcover, pendulous and dwarf forms.

Features: pyramidal or columnar, evergreen tree or shrub; foliage; habit; cones
Height: $1^1/_2$–80' **Spread:** $1^1/_2$–35'
Hardiness: zones 3–8

Holly
Ilex

I. x *meserveae* hybrid (above)
I. x *meserveae* 'Blue Girl' (below)

Hollies vary greatly in shape and size and can be such delights when placed with full consideration for their needs.

Growing

These plants prefer **full sun** but tolerate partial shade. The soil should be of **average to rich fertility, humus rich** and **moist**. Hollies perform best in acidic soil with a pH of 6.5–6.0 or lower. Shelter them from winter wind to help prevent the evergreen leaves from drying out. Apply a summer mulch to keep the roots cool and moist.

Tips

Hollies can be used in groups, in woodland gardens and in shrub and mixed borders. They can also be shaped into hedges. Winterberry is good for naturalizing in moist sites in the garden.

Recommended

I. glabra (inkberry) is a rounded shrub with glossy, deep green, evergreen foliage and dark purple fruit. Cultivars are available. (Zones 4–9)

I. x *meserveae* (meserve holly, blue holly) is a group of hybrids that originated from crosses between tender English holly (*I. aquifolium*) and hardy hollies like prostrate holly (*I. rugosa*). These dense, evergreen shrubs may be erect, mounding or spreading. (Zones 5–8)

I. verticillata (winterberry, winterberry holly) is a deciduous native species grown for its explosion of red fruit that persists into winter. Many cultivars and hybrids are available.

Also called: inkberry, winterberry
Features: erect or spreading, evergreen or deciduous shrub or tree; glossy, sometimes spiny foliage; fruit; habit **Height:** 3–50'
Spread: 3–40' **Hardiness:** zones 3–9

Horsechestnut

Aesculus

Horsechestnuts range from trees with immense regal bearing to small but impressive shrubs. All have spectacular flowers.

Growing

Horsechestnuts grow well in **full sun** or **partial shade**. The soil should be **fertile, moist** and **well drained**. These trees dislike excessive drought.

Tips

Horsechestnuts are used as specimen and shade trees. The roots of horsechestnuts can break up sidewalks and patios if planted too close.

The smaller, shrubby horsechestnuts grow well near pond plantings and also make interesting specimens. Give them plenty of space as they can form large colonies.

Recommended

A. hippocastanum (common horsechestnut) is a large, rounded tree that will branch right to the ground if grown in an open setting. The flowers, white with yellow or pink marks, are borne in long spikes. (Zones 3–7)

A. parviflora (bottlebrush buckeye) is a spreading, mound-forming, suckering shrub that has plentiful spikes of creamy white flowers. (Zones 4–9)

A. pavia (red buckeye) is a low-growing to rounded shrubby tree with cherry red flowers and handsome foliage. It needs consistent moisture. (Zones 4–8)

A. hippocastanum 'Baumanii' (above)
A. hippocastanum (below)

Also called: buckeye **Features:** rounded or spreading, deciduous tree or shrub; early-summer flowers; foliage; spiny fruit
Height: 8–80' **Spread:** 8–65'
Hardiness: zones 3–9

Hydrangea
Hydrangea

H. quercifolia (above), *H. paniculata* 'Grandiflora' (below)

ydrangeas have many attractive qualities, including showy, often long-lasting flowers and glossy green leaves, some of which turn beautiful colors in fall.

Growing

Hydrangeas grow well in **full sun** or **partial shade**, and some species tolerate full shade. Shade or partial shade will reduce leaf and flower scorch in hotter gardens. The soil should be of **average to high fertility, humus rich, moist** and **well drained**. These plants perform best in cool, moist conditions.

Tips

Hydrangeas come in many forms and have many uses in the landscape. They can be included in shrub or mixed borders, used as specimens or informal barriers and planted in groups or containers.

Recommended

H. arborescens (smooth hydrangea) is a rounded shrub that flowers well, even in shady conditions. This species is rarely grown in favor of the cultivars that bear large clusters of showy white blossoms.

H. macrophylla (bigleaf hydrangea) is a rounded shrub that bears flowers in shades of pink, red, blue or purple from mid- to late summer. Many cultivars are available. (Zones 5–9)

H. paniculata (panicle hydrangea) is a spreading to upright large shrub or small tree that bears white flowers from late summer to early fall. **'Grandiflora'** (Peegee hydrangea) is a commonly available cultivar. (Zones 4–8)

H. quercifolia (oakleaf hydrangea) is a mound-forming shrub with attractive, cinnamon brown exfoliating bark, conical clusters of sterile and fertile flowers, and large leaves, which are lobed like an oak's and turn bronze to bright red in fall. (Zones 4–8)

Features: deciduous, mounding or spreading shrub or tree; flowers; habit; foliage; bark
Height: 3–20' **Spread:** 3–10'
Hardiness: zones 3–9

Juniper
Juniperus

J. horizontalis 'Blue Chip' (above), *J. horizontalis* 'Blue Prince' (below)

There may be a juniper in every gardener's future, with all the choices available from low, creeping plants to upright, pyramidal forms.

Growing

Junipers prefer **full sun** but tolerate light shade. Ideally the soil should be of **average fertility** and **well drained**, but these plants tolerate most conditions.

Tips

With the wide variety of junipers available, there are endless uses for them in the garden. They make prickly barriers and hedges, and they can be used in borders, as specimens or in groups. The larger species can be used to form windbreaks, and the low-growing species can be used in rock gardens and as groundcover.

Recommended

Junipers vary, not just from species to species, but often within a species. Cultivars are available for all species and may differ significantly from the species. *J. chinensis* (Chinese juniper) is a conical tree or spreading shrub. *J. horizontalis* (creeping juniper) is a prostrate, creeping groundcover. *J. procumbens* (Japanese garden juniper) is a wide-spreading, stiff-branched, low shrub. *J. scopulorum* (Rocky Mountain juniper) can be upright, rounded, weeping or spreading. *J. squamata* (singleseed juniper) forms a prostrate or low, spreading shrub or a small, upright tree. *J. virginiana* (eastern redcedar) is a durable tree, upright or wide-spreading.

Features: conical or columnar tree, rounded or spreading shrub, prostrate groundcover; evergreen; foliage; variety of colors, sizes and habits **Height:** 4"–80' **Spread:** 18"–25' **Hardiness:** zones 3–9

Lilac

Syringa

S. vulgaris 'Charles Joly' (above), *S. vulgaris* cultivars (below)

The hardest thing about growing lilacs is choosing from the many species and hundreds of cultivars available.

Growing

Lilacs grow best in **full sun**. The soil should be **fertile, humus rich** and **well drained**. These plants tolerate open, windy locations.

Tips

Include lilacs in a shrub or mixed border or use them to create an informal hedge. Japanese tree lilac can be used as a specimen tree.

Recommended

S. x hyacinthiflora (hyacinth-flowered lilac, early-flowering lilac) is a group of hardy, upright hybrids that become spreading as they mature. Clusters of fragrant flowers appear two weeks earlier than those of the French lilacs. The leaves turn reddish purple in fall. Many cultivars are available. (Zones 3–7)

S. meyeri (Meyer lilac) is a compact, rounded shrub that bears fragrant, pink or lavender flowers. (Zones 3–7)

S. reticulata (Japanese tree lilac) is a large, rounded shrub or small tree that bears white flowers. '**Ivory Silk**' has a more compact habit and produces more flowers than the species. (Zones 3–7)

S. vulgaris (French lilac, common lilac) is the plant most people think of when they think of lilacs. It is a suckering, spreading shrub with an irregular habit that bears fragrant, lilac-colored flowers. Hundreds of cultivars with a variety of flower colors are available. (Zones 3–8)

Features: rounded or suckering, deciduous shrub or small tree; late-spring to mid-summer flowers; habit **Height:** 3–30' **Spread:** 3–25' **Hardiness:** zones 2–8

Linden

Tilia

$\mathcal{L}$indens are picturesque shade trees with a signature gumdrop shape and sweet-scented flowers that capture the essence of summer.

Growing

Lindens grow best in **full sun**. The soil should be **average to fertile, moist** and **well drained**. These trees adapt to most pH levels but prefer an alkaline soil. They tolerate pollution and urban conditions.

Tips

Lindens are useful and attractive street trees, shade trees and specimen trees. Their tolerance of pollution and their moderate size make lindens ideal for city gardens.

Recommended

T. cordata (littleleaf linden) is a dense, pyramidal tree that may become rounded with age. It bears small, fragrant flowers with narrow, yellow-green bracts. Cultivars are available.

T. tomentosa (silver linden) has a broad, pyramidal or rounded habit that bears small, fragrant flowers and has glossy green leaves with fuzzy, silvery undersides.

T. cordata (above)

Given enough space to spread, lindens will branch right to the ground.

Features: dense, pyramidal to rounded, deciduous tree; habit; foliage **Height:** 20–65' **Spread:** 15–50' **Hardiness:** zones 3–8

Magnolia
Magnolia

M. x soulangeana (above)

Magnolias are beautiful, fragrant, versatile plants that also provide attractive winter structure.

Growing
Magnolias grow well in **full sun** or **partial shade**. The soil should be **fertile, humus rich, acidic, moist** and **well drained**. A summer mulch will help keep the roots cool and the soil moist.

Tips
Magnolias are used as specimen trees and the smaller species can be used in borders.

Avoid planting magnolias where the morning sun will encourage the blooms to open too early in the season. Cold, wind and rain can damage the blossoms.

Recommended
Many species, hybrids and cultivars, in a range of sizes and with differing flowering times and flower colors, are available. Two of the most common are **M. x soulangeana** (saucer magnolia), a rounded, spreading, deciduous shrub or tree with pink, purple or white flowers; and **M. stellata** (star magnolia), a compact, bushy or spreading, deciduous shrub or small tree with many-petaled, fragrant, white flowers. Check with your local nursery or garden center for other available magnolias.

Features: upright to spreading, deciduous shrub or tree; flowers; fruit; foliage; habit; bark **Height:** 8–40' **Spread:** 5–35' **Hardiness:** zones 3–9

Maple

Acer

Maples are attractive all year, with delicate flowers in spring, attractive foliage and hanging samaras in summer, vibrant leaf color in fall and interesting bark and branch structures in winter.

Growing

Generally, maples do well in **full sun** or **light shade,** though this varies from species to species. The soil should be **fertile, moist, high in organic matter** and **well drained**.

Tips

Maples can be used as specimen trees, as large elements in shrub or mixed borders or as hedges. Some are useful as understory plants bordering wooded areas; others can be grown in containers on patios or terraces. Few Japanese gardens are without the attractive smaller maples. Almost all maples can be used to create bonsai specimens.

Recommended

Maples are some of the most popular trees used as shade or street trees. Many are very large when fully mature, but there are also a few smaller species that are useful in smaller gardens, including **A. campestre** (hedge maple), **A. ginnala** (amur maple), **A. palmatum** (Japanese maple) and **A. rubrum** (red maple). Check with your local nursery or garden center for availability.

A. rubrum (above), A. palmatum var. atropurpureum (below)

Maple wood is hard and dense and is used for fine furniture construction and for some musical instruments.

Features: small, multi-stemmed, deciduous tree or large shrub; foliage; bark; winged fruit; fall color; form; flowers **Height:** 6–80'
Spread: 6–70' **Hardiness:** zones 2–8

Ninebark
Physocarpus

P. opulifolius DIABOLO (above)

This attractive native deserves wider recognition, especially now that cultivars with foliage ranging in color from yellow to purple are available.

Growing
Ninebark grows well in **full sun** or **partial shade**. The best leaf coloring develops in a sunny location. The soil should be **fertile, acidic, moist** and **well drained**.

Tips
Ninebark can be included in a shrub or mixed border, in a woodland garden or in a naturalistic garden.

Recommended
P. opulifolius (common ninebark) is a suckering shrub with long, arching branches and exfoliating bark. It bears light pink flowers in early summer and fruit that ripens to reddish green in fall. Several cultivars with beautifully colored foliage include '**Coppertina,**' '**Dart's Gold,**' DIABOLO, '**Luteus**' and '**Summer Wine.**'

Also called: common ninebark
Features: upright, sometimes suckering, deciduous shrub; early-summer flowers; fruit; bark; foliage **Height:** 4–10' **Spread:** 4–15'
Hardiness: zones 2–8

Oak
Quercus

The oak's classic shape, outstanding fall color, deep roots and long life are some of its many assets. Plant it for its individual beauty and for posterity.

Growing

Oaks grow well in **full sun** or **partial shade**. The soil should be **fertile, moist** and **well drained**. These trees can be difficult to establish; transplant them only while they are young.

Tips

Oaks are large trees that are best used as specimens or for groves in parks and large gardens. Do not disturb the ground around the base of an oak; this tree is very sensitive to changes in grade.

Recommended

There are many oaks to choose from. A few popular species are **Q. alba** (white oak), a rounded, spreading tree with peeling bark and purple-red fall color; **Q. coccinea** (scarlet oak), noted for having the most brilliant red fall color of all the oaks; **Q. robur** (English oak), a rounded, spreading tree with golden yellow fall color; and **Q. rubra** (red oak), a rounded, spreading tree with fall color ranging from yellow to red-brown. Some cultivars are available. Check with your local nursery or garden center.

Q. *robur* (above & below)

Although acorns are generally not edible, acorns of certain oak species are edible but usually must be processed first to leach out the bitter tannins.

Features: large, rounded, spreading, deciduous tree; summer and fall foliage; bark; habit; acorns **Height:** 35–120' **Spread:** 10–100' **Hardiness:** zones 3–9

Pine
Pinus

P. mugo (above), *P. strobus* (below)

The Austrian pine, P. nigra, was often recommended as the most urban-tolerant pine, but overplanting has led to severe disease problems, some of which can kill a tree in a single growing season.

Pines offer exciting possibilities for any garden. Exotic-looking pines are available with soft or stiff needles, needles with yellow bands, trunks with patterned or mother-of-pearl-like bark and varied forms.

Growing
Pines grow best in **full sun**. These trees adapt to most **well-drained** soils but do not tolerate polluted urban conditions.

Tips
Pines can be used as specimen trees, as hedges or to create windbreaks. Smaller cultivars can be included in shrub or mixed borders. These trees are not heavy feeders; fertilizing will encourage rapid new growth that is weak and susceptible to pest and disease problems.

Recommended
There are many available pines, both trees and shrubby dwarf plants. Check with your local garden center or nursery to see what is available. Two excellent choices are **P. wallichiana** (Himalayan pine), a magnificent specimen tree with long, silky blue-green needles, which can grow to be over 110' tall in the wild; and **P. flexilis 'Vanderwolf's Pyramid,'** a fast-growing, adaptable, shade-tolerant, upright pine well suited to our area.

Features: upright, columnar or spreading, evergreen tree; foliage; bark; cones; habit
Height: 2–120' **Spread:** 2–60'
Hardiness: zones 2–8

Potentilla
Potentilla

Potentilla is a fuss-free shrub that blooms madly all summer. The cheery, yellow-flowered variety is often seen, but cultivars with flowers in shades of pink, red and tangerine have broadened the use of this reliable shrub.

Growing
Potentilla prefers **full sun** but tolerates partial or light shade. The soil should preferably be of **poor to average fertility** and **well drained**. This plant tolerates most conditions, including sandy or clay soil and wet or dry conditions. Established plants are drought tolerant. Too much fertilizer or too rich a soil will encourage weak, floppy, disease-prone growth.

Tips
Potentilla is useful in a shrub or mixed border. The smaller cultivars can be included in rock gardens and on rock walls. On slopes that are steep or awkward to mow, potentilla can prevent soil erosion and reduce the time spent maintaining the lawn. It can even be used to form a low, informal hedge.

If your potentilla's flowers fade in the bright sun or in hot weather, try moving the plant to a more sheltered location. A cooler location that still gets a lot of sun or a spot with some shade from the hot afternoon sun may be all your plant needs to keep its color. Colors should revive in fall as the weather cools. Yellow-flowered plants are the least likely to be affected by heat and sun.

P. fruticosa 'Tangerine' (above), *P. fruticosa* (below)

Recommended
Of the many cultivars of *P. fruticosa,* the following are a few of the most popular and interesting. **'Abbotswood'** is one of the best white-flowered cultivars, **'Pink Beauty'** bears pink, semi-double flowers, **'Tangerine'** has orange flowers and **'Yellow Gem'** has bright yellow flowers.

Also called: shrubby cinquefoil
Features: mounding, deciduous shrub; flowers; foliage; habit **Height:** 12–60"
Spread: 12–60" **Hardiness:** zones 2–8

Redbud

Cercis

Redbud is an outstanding treasure of spring. Deep magenta flowers bloom before the leaves emerge, and their impact is intense. As the buds open, the flowers turn pink, covering the long, thin branches in vibrant clouds.

Growing

Redbud will grow well in **full sun, partial shade** or **light shade**. The soil should be a **fertile, deep loam** that is **moist** and **well drained**. This plant has tender roots and does not like being transplanted.

Tips

Redbud can be used as a specimen tree, in a shrub or mixed border or in a woodland garden. It tends to self-seed and can be short-lived.

Recommended

C. canadensis (eastern redbud) is a spreading, multi-stemmed tree that bears red, purple or pink flowers. The young foliage is bronze, fading to green over summer and turning bright yellow in fall. Many beautiful cultivars are available.

C. canadensis (above & below)

Redbud is not as long-lived as many other trees, so use its delicate beauty to supplement more permanent trees in the garden.

Features: rounded or spreading, multi-stemmed, deciduous tree or shrub; spring flowers; fall foliage **Height:** 20–30' **Spread:** 25–35' **Hardiness:** zones 4–9

Rhododendron

Rhododendron

Even when not covered in a stunning display of brightly colored flowers, rhododendrons are wonderful landscape plants.

Growing
Rhododendrons and evergreen azaleas grow best in **partial shade** or **light shade,** while the deciduous azaleas typically grow best in full sun or partial shade. Choose a location that is protected from drying winter winds. The soil should be **fertile, humus rich, acidic, moist** and **well drained**. A good mulch is important to keep the soil moist and protect the shallow roots of these plants.

Tips
Rhododendrons and azaleas perform best and look good when planted in groups. Use them in shrub or mixed borders, in woodland gardens and in sheltered rock gardens.

Recommended
These bushy shrubs vary greatly in size and hardiness. They may be evergreen or deciduous and bear flowers in a huge range of colors. There are hundreds of rhododendron and azalea species, hybrids and cultivars available. Visit your local garden center or specialty grower to see what is available.

R. 'Purple Gem' (above), Azalea hybrid (below)

Rhododendrons and azaleas are grouped together in the genus Rhododendron. *Extensive breeding and hybridizing is making it more difficult to apply one name or the other to many plants.*

Also called: azalea **Features:** upright, mounding, rounded, evergreen or deciduous shrub; late-winter to early-summer flowers; foliage; habit **Height:** 24"–12'
Spread: 24"–12' **Hardiness:** zones 3–8

Serviceberry
Amelanchier

A. canadensis (above)

*T*he *Amelanchier* species are first-rate North American natives, bearing lacy, white flowers in spring, followed by edible berries. In fall the foliage color ranges from a glowing apricot to deep red.

Growing
Serviceberries grow well in **full sun** or **light shade**. They prefer **acidic soil** that is **fertile, humus rich, moist** and **well drained**. They do adjust to drought.

Tips
With spring flowers, edible fruit, attractive leaves that turn red in fall and often artistic branch growth, serviceberries make beautiful specimen plants or even shade trees in small gardens. The shrubbier forms can be grown along the edges of a woodland or in a border. In the wild, these trees are often found growing near water sources and are beautiful beside ponds or streams.

Recommended
Several species and hybrids are available. A few popular serviceberries are *A. arborea* (downy serviceberry, Juneberry), a small, single- or multi-stemmed tree; *A. canadensis* (shadblow serviceberry), a large, upright, suckering shrub; and *A.* x *grandiflora* (apple serviceberry), a small, spreading, often multi-stemmed tree. All three have white flowers, purple fruit and good fall color.

Also called: saskatoon, juneberry
Features: single- or multi-stemmed, deciduous, large shrub or small tree; spring or early-summer flowers; edible fruit; fall color; habit; bark **Height:** 4–30' **Spread:** 4–30'
Hardiness: zones 3–9

Seven-Son Flower
Heptacodium

As a smallish tree with fragrant, white, September flowers followed by red sepals and fruit, seven-son flower makes a welcome addition to our plant palette.

Growing

Seven-son flower prefers **full sun** but tolerates partial shade. The soil should be of **average fertility, moist** and **well drained**, though this plant is fairly tolerant of most soil conditions, including dry and acidic soil.

Tips

This large shrub can be used in place of a shade tree on a small property. Planted near a patio or deck, the plant will provide light shade, and its fragrant flowers can be enjoyed in late summer. In a border it provides light shade to plants growing below it, and the dark green leaves make a good backdrop for bright perennial and annual flowers.

Seven-son flower's tolerance of dry and salty soils makes it useful where salty snow may be shoveled off walkways in winter and where watering will be minimal in summer.

Recommended

H. miconioides is a large, multi-stemmed shrub or small tree with peeling tan bark and dark green leaves that may become tinged with purple in fall. Clusters of fragrant, creamy white flowers have persistent sepals (the outer ring of flower parts) that turn dark pink to bright red in mid- to late fall and surround small, purple-red fruit.

H. miconioides (above & below)

This plant is a fairly recent introduction to North American gardens and may not be available in all garden centers.

Features: upright to spreading, multi-stemmed, deciduous shrub or small tree; habit; bark; fall flowers **Height:** 15–20' **Spread:** 8–15' **Hardiness:** zones 5–8

Smokebush

Cotinus

C. coggygria 'Royal Purple' (above), *C. coggygria* (below)

Growing

Smokebush grows well in **full sun** or **partial shade**. It prefers soil of **average fertility** that is **moist** and **well drained**, but it adapts to all but very wet soils.

Tips

Smokebush can be used in a shrub or mixed border, as a single specimen or in groups. It is a good choice for a rocky hillside planting. Shrubs grown for their colorful foliage can be cut back to the ground each spring; they will not flower, but foliage color will be intensified.

Recommended

C. coggygria is a bushy, rounded shrub that develops large, puffy plumes of flowers that start out green and gradually turn a pinky gray. The green foliage turns red, orange and yellow in fall. Many cultivars are available, including reddish purple or purple-leaved selections like **'Notcutt's Variety,'** **'Royal Purple,'** and **'Velvet Cloak,'** as well as yellow-leaved selections like GOLDEN SPIRIT (**'Ancot'**), the foliage of which turns orange, red and coral pink in fall.

C. obovatus (American smokebush, chittamwood) is our native smokebush that grows 20–30' tall. It is an upright tree with blue-green leaves that turn spectacular shades of yellow, orange, red and violet in fall.

Bright fall color, adaptability, flowers of differing colors, and variable sizes and forms make smokebush and all its cultivars excellent additions to the garden.

Also called: smoketree **Features:** bushy, rounded, spreading, deciduous tree or shrub; early-summer flowers; summer and fall foliage **Height:** 10–15' **Spread:** 10–15' **Hardiness:** zones 4–8

Snowbell
Styrax

S. *obassia* (above)

Snowbells are easy to admire for their delicate, shapely appearance and dangling flowers clustered along the undersides of the branches.

Growing
Snowbells grow well in **full sun, partial shade** or **light shade**. The soil should be **fertile, humus rich, neutral to acidic, moist** and **well drained**.

Tips
Snowbells can be used to provide light shade in shrub or mixed borders. They can also be included in woodland gardens, and they make interesting specimens near entryways or patios.

Recommended
S. obassia (fragrant snowbell) is a broad, columnar tree that bears white flowers in long clusters at the branch ends in early summer. *S. japonica* (Japanese snowbell) is another commonly available species, but it is not recommended because it is becoming invasive in native forests.

Features: upright, rounded, spreading or columnar, deciduous tree; late-spring to early-summer flowers; foliage; habit **Height:** 20–40' **Spread:** 20–30' **Hardiness:** zones 4–8

Spirea
Spiraea

S. japonica 'Little Princess' (above), *S. x vanhouttei* (below)

Spireas, seen in so many gardens and with dozens of cultivars, remain undeniable favorites. With a wide range of forms, sizes and colors of both foliage and flowers, spireas have many possible uses in the landscape.

Growing

Spireas prefer **full sun**, but to help prevent foliage burn, provide protection from very hot afternoon sun. The soil should be **fertile, acidic, moist** and **well drained**.

Tips

Spireas are used in shrub or mixed borders, in rock gardens and as informal screens and hedges.

Recommended

Many species and cultivars of spirea are available. The following are a few popular hybrid groups. *S. japonica* (*S. x bumalda*) is a low, broad, mounded shrub with pink flowers. It is rarely grown in favor of the many cultivars, which also have pink flowers but often with brightly colored foliage. *S. thunbergii* (thunberg spirea) is a dense, bushy shrub with arching stems, light green foliage and white, spring to early-summer flowers. **'Fujino Pink'** has light pink flowers. MELLO YELLOW (**'Ogon'**) has bright yellow foliage that is tinged with orange and pink in the summer. *S. x vanhouttei* (bridal wreath spirea, Vanhoutte spirea) is a dense, bushy shrub with arching branches that bears clusters of white flowers. Check with your local nursery or garden center to see what cultivars are available.

Features: round, bushy, deciduous shrub; summer flowers; habit **Height:** 1–10' **Spread:** 1–12' **Hardiness:** zones 3–9

Spruce
Picea

P. abies 'Nidiformis' (above), *P. pungens* var. *glauca* 'Moerheim' (below)

Spruce is one of the most commonly grown and commonly abused evergreens. Grow spruces where they have enough room to spread, then let them branch all the way to the ground.

Growing

Spruce trees grow best in **full sun**. The soil should be **deep, moist, well drained** and **neutral to acidic**. These trees generally don't like hot, dry or polluted conditions. Spruces are best grown from small, young stock as they dislike being transplanted when larger or more mature.

Tips

Spruces are used as specimen trees. The dwarf and slow-growing cultivars can also be used in shrub or mixed borders. These trees look most attractive when allowed to keep their lower branches.

Recommended

Spruces are generally upright, pyramidal trees, but cultivars may be low-growing, wide-spreading or even weeping in habit. *P. abies* (Norway spruce), *P. glauca* (white spruce), *P. omorika* (Serbian spruce), *P. pungens* (Colorado spruce) and their cultivars are popular and commonly available.

Features: conical or columnar, evergreen tree or shrub; foliage; cones; habit **Height:** 2–80'
Spread: 2–25' **Hardiness:** zones 2–8

Stewartia
Stewartia

*T*his lovely tree adds beauty to your garden year-round, with dark green summer foliage, summer flowers, colorful fall foliage and exfoliating bark.

Growing
Stewartia grows well in **full sun** or **light shade**. The soil should be of **average to high fertility, humus rich, neutral to acidic, moist** and **well drained**. Provide shelter from strong winds. Transplant these trees when they are very young as the roots resent being disturbed.

Tips
Stewartia is used as a specimen tree and in group plantings. It makes a good companion for rhododendrons and azaleas because stewartia will provide the light shade they enjoy, and all these plants grow well in similar soil conditions.

Recommended
S. pseudocamellia is a broad, columnar or pyramidal tree. White flowers with showy yellow stamens appear in mid-summer. The dark green leaves turn shades of yellow, orange, scarlet and reddish purple in fall. The bark is scaly and exfoliating, leaving the trunk mottled with gray, orange, pink and reddish brown. Cultivars are available.

Don't be concerned if the bark doesn't put on a display when you first plant your stewartia. It takes several years for the tree to mature enough for the flaking to develop.

Also called: Japanese stewartia
Features: broad, conical or rounded, deciduous tree; mid-summer flowers; summer and fall foliage; exfoliating bark **Height:** 20–35'
Spread: 20–35' **Hardiness:** zones 5–7

Summersweet Clethra

Clethra

Summersweet clethra is one of the best shrubs for adding fragrance to your garden and for attracting butterflies and other pollinators.

Growing

Summersweet clethra grows best in **light or partial shade**. The soil should be **fertile, humus rich, acidic, moist** and **well drained**.

Tips

Although not aggressive, this shrub tends to sucker, forming a colony of stems. Use it in a border or in a woodland garden. The light shade along the edge of a woodland is also an ideal location.

Recommended

C. alnifolia is a large, rounded, upright, colony-forming shrub. It grows 38' tall, spreading 3–6', and bears attractive spikes of white flowers in mid- to late summer. The foliage turns yellow in fall. Several cultivars are available, including pink-flowered selections.

C. alnifolia 'Paniculata' (above & below)

Summersweet clethra is useful in damp, shaded gardens, where the late-season flowers are much appreciated.

Also called: sweet pepperbush, sweetspire
Features: rounded, suckering deciduous shrub; fragrant, summer flowers; attractive habit; colorful fall foliage **Height:** 2–8'
Spread: 3–8' **Hardiness:** zones 3–9

Viburnum
Viburnum

V. opulus (above)
V. plicatum var. tomentosum (below)

These plants will look neatest if dead-headed, but this practice will prevent fruits from forming. Fruiting is better when more than one plant of a species is grown.

Tips
Viburnums can be used in borders and woodland gardens. They are a good choice for plantings near swimming pools.

Recommended
Many viburnum species, hybrids and cultivars are available. A few popular ones include **V. carlesii** (Korean spice viburnum), a dense, bushy, rounded, deciduous shrub with white or pink, spice-scented flowers (zones 5–8); **V. opulus** (European cranberrybush, Guelder-rose), a rounded, spreading, deciduous shrub with lacy-looking flower clusters (zones 3–8); **V. plicatum var. tomentosum** (doublefile viburnum), with a graceful, horizontal branching pattern that gives the shrub a layered effect and lacy-looking, white flower clusters (zones 5–8); **V. setigerum,** a deciduous, multi-stemmed, upright, leggy shrub with white flowers in spring. It grows slowly to 8–12' tall, 5' wide, and has showy orange fruit against russet foliage in fall; and **V. trilobum** (American cranberrybush, highbush cranberry), a dense, rounded shrub with clusters of white flowers followed by edible, red fruit (zones 2–7).

Good fall color, attractive form, shade tolerance, scented flowers and attractive fruit put the viburnums in a class by themselves.

Growing
Viburnums grow well in **full sun, partial shade** or **light shade**. The soil should be of **average fertility, moist** and **well drained**. Viburnums tolerate both alkaline and acidic soils.

Features: bushy or spreading, evergreen, semi-evergreen or deciduous shrub; flowers (some fragrant); summer and fall foliage; fruit; habit **Height:** 1^1/$_2$–20' **Spread:** 1^1/$_2$–15' **Hardiness:** zones 2–8

Weigela
Weigela

W. florida 'Siebold Variegata' (above), *W. florida* culivar (below)

Weigelas have been improved through breeding, and specimens with more compact forms, longer flowering periods and greater cold tolerance are now available.

Growing

Weigelas prefer **full sun** but tolerate partial shade. The soil should be **fertile** and **well drained**. These plants will adapt to most well-drained soil conditions.

Tips

Weigelas can be used in shrub or mixed borders, in open woodland gardens and as informal barrier plantings.

Recommended

W. florida is a spreading shrub with arching branches that bears clusters of dark pink flowers. Many hybrids and cultivars are available, including dwarf varieties, varieties with red, pink or white flowers, and varieties with purple, bronze or yellow foliage. **'Variegata'** has white margined leaves and lightly fragrant, pink flowers. WINE & ROSES has striking burgundy leaves and magenta blossoms.

Features: upright or low, spreading, deciduous shrub; late-spring to early-summer flowers; foliage; habit **Height:** 1–9' **Spread:** 1–12' **Hardiness:** zones 3–8

Willow

Salix

S. *integra* 'Hakuro Nishiki' (above)

Tips

Large tree willows should be reserved for large spaces and are particularly attractive near water features. Smaller willows can be used as small specimen trees or in shrub and mixed borders. Small and trailing forms can be included in rock gardens and along retaining walls.

Recommended

The following are just a few of the many popular willows available.

S. alba 'Tristis' is a deciduous, rounded tree with delicate, flexible, weeping branches. The young growth and fall leaves are bright yellow. (Zones 4–8)

S. x *grahamii* (Graham's willow) is a shrubby dwarf hybrid. A low, trailing cultivar is available.

S. integra 'Hakuro Nishiki' (dappled willow, Japanese dappled willow) is a spreading shrub with supple, arching branches that appear almost weeping. The young shoots are orange-pink in color and the leaves are dappled green, cream and pink. (Zones 5–8)

S. SCARLET CURLS (*S.* 'Sarcuzam') is an upright, shrubby tree with curled and twisted branches and leaves. The young stems are reddish and become redder after a frost, creating an attractive winter display of twisted red shoots. (Zones 5–8)

These fast-growing deciduous shrubs or trees can have colorful or twisted stems or foliage, and they come in a huge range of growth habits and sizes.

Growing

Willows grow best in **full sun**. The soil should be of **average fertility, moist** and **well drained**, though some of the shrubby species are drought resistant.

Features: bushy or arching shrub, or spreading or weeping tree; summer and fall foliage; stems; habit **Height:** 1–65' **Spread:** 3–65' **Hardiness:** zones 3–8

Witchhazel
Hamamelis

Witchhazel is an investment in happiness. It blooms in early spring, the flowers last for weeks, and their spicy fragrance awakens the senses. Then in fall, the handsome leaves develop overlapping bands of orange, yellow and red.

Growing
Witchhazel grows best in a sheltered spot with **full sun** or **light shade**. The soil should be of **average fertility, neutral to acidic, moist** and **well drained**.

Tips
Witchhazel works well individually or in groups. It can be used as a specimen plant, in shrub or mixed borders or in woodland gardens. As a small tree, it is ideal for space-limited gardens.

The unique flowers have long, narrow, crinkled petals that give the plant a spidery appearance when in bloom. If the weather gets too cold, the petals will roll up, protecting the flowers and extending the flowering season.

Recommended
H. x *intermedia* is a vase-shaped, spreading shrub that bears fragrant clusters of yellow, orange or red flowers. The leaves turn attractive shades of orange, red and bronze in fall. Cultivars with flowers in shades of red, yellow or orange are available.

Features: spreading, deciduous shrub or small tree; fragrant, early-spring flowers; summer and fall foliage; habit **Height:** 6–20'
Spread: 6–20' **Hardiness:** zones 5–9

Yew
Taxus

T. x *media* 'Sunburst' (above)

Growing

Yews grow well in any light condition from **full sun to full shade**. The soil should be **fertile, moist** and **well drained**. These trees tolerate windy, dry and polluted conditions and soils of any acidity. They dislike excessive heat, however, and on the hotter south or southwest side of a building they may suffer needle scorch.

Tips

Yews can be used in borders or as specimens, hedges, topiaries and groundcovers.

Male and female flowers are borne on separate plants. Both must be present for the attractive red arils (seed cups) to form.

From sweeping hedges to commanding specimens, yews serve many purposes in the garden. They are the only reliable evergreens for deep shade.

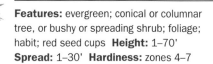

Recommended

T. x *media* (English Japanese yew), a cross between *T. baccata* (English yew) and *T. cuspidata* (Japanese yew), has the vigor of the English yew and the cold hardiness of the Japanese yew. It forms a rounded, upright tree or shrub, though the size and form can vary among the many cultivars.

Features: evergreen; conical or columnar tree, or bushy or spreading shrub; foliage; habit; red seed cups **Height:** 1–70'
Spread: 1–30' **Hardiness:** zones 4–7

Apothecary's Rose
Species Rose

This rose has been cultivated since the 13th century and was used in herbal medicine to treat inflammation, aches and pains and insomnia.

Growing
Apothecary's Rose prefers **full sun** but tolerates afternoon shade. The soil should be **average to fertile, slightly acidic, humus rich, moist** and **well drained**. The suckers it produces should be removed once flowering is complete.

Tips
Apothecary's Rose can be grown as a specimen, in a shrub border or as a hedge. It can be naturalized or used to prevent soil erosion on a bank too steep for mowing. The flowers are very fragrant; plant this shrub near windows, doors and frequently used pathways.

Recommended
Rosa gallica 'Officinalis' is a bushy, rounded, vigorous, disease-resistant shrub with bristly stems and dark green leaves. One flush of semi-double flowers is produced each year in late spring or early summer. *Rosa gallica* 'Versicolor' has white or light pink flowers with darker pink splashes and stripes.

R. gallica 'Versicolor' (above), R. gallica 'Officinalis' (below)

This rose is known for its culinary and medicinal value and its use in crafts, particularly in potpourri.
This species rose may self-seed.

Also called: red damask, red rose of Lancaster
Features: rounded habit; fresh and intensely fragrant, early-summer flowers; dark red hips
Flower color: crimson purple to pinkish red
Height: 3$^{1}/_{2}$–4' **Spread:** 3$^{1}/_{2}$–4'
Hardiness: zones 3–10

Blush Noisette

Old Garden Rose

Noisette roses are sometimes classi-fied as old garden roses and some-times as climbing roses.

Growing

Blush Noisette grows best in **full sun** but tolerates light shade. The soil should be **average to fertile, humus rich, slightly acidic, moist** and **well drained**, but it tolerates most soil conditions once established.

Old garden roses are those that were discovered or hybridized before 1867, and they are admired for their delicate beauty, old-fashioned appearance and fantastic fragrance. They are the ancestors of many roses found today.

Tips

Old garden roses like Blush Noisette seem most at home in a country-style garden but can be used in formal and informal borders and as specimens. As a specimen, Blush Noisette will be quite shrubby in habit, but it will perform well as a climber when trained to grow up a wall, fence or arbor.

Recommended

Rosa 'Blush Noisette' is a vigorous shrub with glossy, green foliage. Clusters of spicy, clove-scented, pink-flushed, white flowers that open from pink buds are produced in clusters from early summer to fall.

Also called: noisette carnée **Features:** foliage; habit; fragrant flowers **Flower color:** white flushed with pink **Height:** 4–8' **Spread:** 4–8' **Hardiness:** zones 6–9

Carefree Wonder

Modern Shrub Rose

The name of this shrub rose is perfectly appropriate; it requires very little care and produces copious quantities of flowers in waves throughout summer.

Growing

Carefree Wonder prefers **full sun** but tolerates some shade. The soil should be **average to fertile, humus rich, slightly acidic, moist** and **well drained**, but this rose has proven to be quite adaptable to a variety of soil conditions. Carefree Wonder is disease resistant. Deadhead to encourage blooming.

Tips

Carefree Wonder makes a good addition to a mixed bed or border, and it is attractive when planted in groups. It can also be mass planted to create a large display or grown singly, as an equally attractive specimen.

Recommended

Rosa **'Carefree Wonder'** is a bushy, rounded shrub with glossy, dark green, deeply serrated foliage. Clusters of double pink flowers with silvery undersides to the petals are borne for most of the summer. There are several other roses in the **'Carefree'** series, including **'Carefree Beauty'** with medium pink double flowers and **'Carefree Sunshine'** with yellow flowers.

'Carefree Wonder' (above & below)

The color of the flowers varies with the weather and the age of the bloom, ranging through bright and light shades of pink.

Also called: Dynastie **Features:** rounded habit; summer foliage, long blooming period; attractive orange hips; disease resistant
Flower color: variable shades of pink
Height: 3–5' **Spread:** 3–5'
Hardiness: zones 4–9

Flower Carpet

Groundcover Rose

Since their release in 1991, the Flower Carpet roses have proven themselves to be low-maintenance, black-spot–resistant, long-blooming performers in the landscape.

Growing

Flower Carpet roses grow best in **full sun**. The soil should be **average to fertile, humus rich, slightly acidic, moist** and **well drained**, but this hardy rose is fairly adaptable.

Tips

Although not true groundcovers, these small shrub roses have dense and spreading habits useful for filling in large areas. They can also be used as low hedges or in mixed borders. Their sometimes long, rangy canes may require some pruning to reduce their spread. Flower Carpet roses even grow well near roads, sidewalks and driveways where salt is applied in winter.

Recommended

Rosa '**Flower Carpet**' roses are bushy, low-growing, spreading plants with shiny, bright green, leathery foliage. They produce single or semi-double flowers in white, yellow, pink, coral, red, or apple-blossom, with prominent yellow stamens. These flowers last from early summer through fall to the first heavy frost.

Features: mounding, spreading habit; summer through fall flowers **Flower color:** deep hot pink, yellow, white, coral, red, apple-blossom **Height:** 30–36" **Spread:** 3–4' **Hardiness:** zones 5–9

Golden Celebration

English (David Austin) Shrub Rose

David Austin roses are famous for their scent, and Golden Celebration is no exception. The fruity smell of these flowers is strong enough to catch the attention of any passerby.

Growing

Golden Celebration grows best in **full sun** in a **warm, sheltered location**. The soil should be **fertile, humus rich, slightly acidic, moist** and **well drained**. Deadhead to keep the plants tidy and to encourage continuous blooming. Protection may be required to overwinter this rose successfully.

Tips

David Austin roses such as Golden Celebration have many uses and are often included in borders or as specimens. With training, Golden Celebration can also be used as a climber. Plant it near a window, door or pathway where its fragrance can best be enjoyed.

Recommended

Rosa **'Golden Celebration'** forms a rounded shrub with dark green, glossy foliage and flexible canes that sway or bend under the weight of the double flowers. Golden Celebration is one of many Austin roses that are also available in shades of pink, orange, apricot, yellow or white.

Golden Celebration is considered one of the largest-flowered and most stunning David Austin roses ever developed.

Features: attractive rounded habit; fruit-scented, early summer to fall flowers **Flower color:** golden yellow, pink, orange, apricot, yellow, white **Height:** 4–5' **Spread:** 4–5' **Hardiness:** zones 5–9

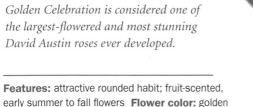

Hansa

Rugosa Shrub Rose

Hansa, first introduced in 1905, is one of the most durable, long-lived and versatile roses.

Growing

Hansa grows best in **full sun**. The soil should preferably be **average to fertile, humus rich, slightly acidic, moist** and **well drained,** but this durable rose adapts to most soils, from sandy to silty clay. Remove a few of the oldest canes every few years to keep plants blooming vigorously.

Tips

Rugosa roses like Hansa make good additions to mixed borders and beds, and can also be used as hedges or as specimens. They are often used on steep banks to prevent soil erosion. Their prickly branches deter people from walking across flower beds and compacting the soil.

Recommended

Rosa '**Hansa**' is a bushy shrub with arching canes and leathery, deeply veined, bright green leaves. The double flowers are produced all summer. The bright orange hips persist into winter. Other rugosa roses include '**Blanc Double de Coubert**,' which produces white, double flowers all summer.

Rosa rugosa is a wide-spreading plant with disease-resistant foliage, a trait it has passed on to many hybrids and cultivars.

Features: dense, arching habit; clove-scented, early-summer to fall flowers; orange-red hips **Flower color:** mauve purple or mauve red **Height:** 4–5' **Spread:** 5–6' **Hardiness:** zones 3–9

Iceberg
Floribunda Rose

Over 40 years have passed since this exceptional rose was first introduced into commerce, and its continued popularity proves it can stand the test of time.

Growing
Iceberg grows best in **full sun**. The soil should be **fertile, humus rich, slightly acidic, moist** and **well drained**.

Tips
Iceberg is a popular addition to mixed borders and beds, and also works well as a specimen. Plant it in a well-used area or near a window where the fragrance of its flowers can best be enjoyed. This rose can also be included in large planters or patio containers.

Recommended
Rosa 'Iceberg' is a vigorous shrub with a rounded, bushy habit and light green foliage. The clusters of semi-double flowers are produced in several flushes from early to mid-summer. A climbing variation of this rose is also available.

Iceberg blooms tend to be flushed with pink when the nights are cool. Rain or dewdrops on the petals can also stain the petals pink.

Also called: fée des neiges **Features:** bushy habit; strong, sweet fragrance; early to mid-summer flowers **Flower color:** white, sometimes flushed with pink during cool or wet weather **Height:** 3–4' **Spread:** 3–4' **Hardiness:** zones 5–9

Knockout
Modern Shrub Rose

This rose is simply one of the best new shrub roses to hit the market in years.

Growing
Knockout grows best in **full sun**. The soil should be **fertile, humus rich, slightly acidic, moist** and **well drained**. This rose blooms most prolifically in warm weather but has deeper red flowers in cooler weather. Deadhead lightly to keep the plant tidy and to encourage prolific blooming.

Tips
This vigorous, attractive rose makes a good addition to a mixed bed or border, and it is attractive when planted in groups of three or more. It can be mass planted to create a large display or grown singly, as an equally attractive specimen.

If you've been afraid that roses need too much care, you'll appreciate the hardiness and disease resistance of this low-maintenance beauty.

Recommended
Rosa 'Knockout' has an attractive, rounded form with glossy, green leaves that turn to shades of burgundy in fall. The bright cherry red flowers are borne in clusters of 3–15 almost all summer and into fall. Orange-red hips last well into winter. You can also get '**Double Knockout**,' '**Pink Knockout**' and a light pink selection called '**Blushing Knockout**.' All have excellent disease resistance.

Also called: Knock out **Features:** rounded habit; light tea-rose-scented, mid-summer to fall flowers; disease resistant **Flower color:** cherry red, light pink **Height:** 3–4' **Spread:** 3–4' **Hardiness:** zones 4–10

New Dawn
Climbing Rose

*I*ntroduced in 1930, New Dawn is still a favorite climbing rose of gardeners and rosarians alike.

Growing
New Dawn grows best in **full sun**. The soil should be **average to fertile, humus rich, slightly acidic, moist** and **well drained**. This rose is disease resistant.

Tips
Train New Dawn to climb pergolas, walls, pillars, arbors, trellises and fences. With some judicious pruning, this rose can be trained to form a bushy shrub or hedge. Plant this rose where the summer-long profusion of blooms will welcome visitors to your home.

Recommended
Rosa 'New Dawn' is a vigorous climber with upright, arching canes and glossy, green foliage. It bears pale pink flowers, singly or in small clusters.

New Dawn was inducted into the World Federation of Rose Societies' Hall of Fame in 1997.

Features: glossy, green foliage; climbing habit; long blooming period; flowers with a sweet, apple-like fragrance **Flower color:** pale pearl pink **Height:** 10–15' **Spread:** 10–15' **Hardiness:** zones 4–9

Rosa glauca
Species Rose

This species rose is a gardener's dream; it's hardy and disease resistant with striking foliage in summer and colorful hips in winter.

Growing
Rosa glauca grows best and develops contrasting foliage color in **full sun** but tolerates some shade. The soil should be **average to fertile, humus rich, slightly acidic, moist** and **well drained**, but this rose adapts to most soils, from sandy soil to silty clay.

Remove a few of the oldest canes to the ground every few years to encourage younger, more colorful stems to grow in. Removing spent flowers won't prolong the blooming period; the more flowers you leave, the more hips will form.

Tips
With its unusual foliage color, Rosa glauca makes a good addition to mixed borders and beds, and it can also be used as a hedge or specimen.

Recommended
Rosa glauca (*R. rubrifolia*) is a bushy shrub with arching, purple-tinged canes and delicate, purple-tinged, blue-green leaves. The single, star-like flowers bloom in clusters in late spring. The dark red hips persist until spring.

Also called: red-leaved rose **Features:** dense, arching habit; purple- or red-tinged foliage; late-spring flowers; persistent, dark red hips **Flower color:** mauve pink with white centers **Height:** 6–10' **Spread:** 5–6' **Hardiness:** zones 2–9

Ruby Pendant
Miniature Rose

The mention of miniature roses brings to mind diminutive plants with dainty flowers, and though Ruby Pendant's flowers are indeed miniature, the plant itself is in no way diminutive.

Growing
Ruby Pendant grows best in **full sun**. The soil should be **fertile, humus rich, slightly acidic, moist** and **well drained**. Deadhead to keep plants neat and encourage continuous blooming.

Tips
Ruby Pendant can be included in planters and mixed containers. In a bed or border it can be planted in groups or individually to accentuate specific areas. It can also be used to create a low hedge. The habit is more like that of a climbing rose than a miniature, and it can be trained as such to grow on a low fence or wall.

Recommended
Rosa **'Ruby Pendant'** is a compact, bushy shrub with reddish green foliage. It produces solitary double flowers all summer.

Features: bushy habit; slightly fragrant, early-summer to fall flowers **Flower color:** red-purple **Height:** 3–4' **Spread:** 24" **Hardiness:** zones 5–8

This unique rose was first introduced in 1979, and the lovely blooms are frequent winners at rose shows and in the garden.

Scentimental

Floribunda Rose

The red and white striped flowers of Scentimental are almost as alluring as their spicy fragrance.

Growing

Scentimental grows best in **full sun** in a **warm, sheltered location**. Soil should be **fertile, humus-rich, slightly acidic, moist** and **well drained**. This rose likes a very fertile soil; amending the soil with additional **organic matter** will improve its nutrient content, texture, water retention and drainage. Winter protection will help this rose overwinter successfully.

Tips

Scentimental has a neat rounded form that makes it an excellent specimen plant as well as a lovely addition to a mixed border.

Recommended

Rosa 'Scentimental' is a shrubby, rounded rose with large dark green leaves. It produces fully double flowers all summer.

Scentimental was an All-America Rose Selection in 1997 and is admired for its disease resistance, vigor, habit and stunning fragrant flowers.

Features: shrubby habit; red and white striped summer to fall flowers
Height: 3–4' **Spread:** 3–4'
Hardiness: zones 4–9

Black-Eyed Susan Vine

Thunbergia

Black-eyed Susan vine is a useful flowering vine whose simple flowers dot the plant, giving it a cheerful, welcoming appearance.

Growing

Black-eyed Susan vines do well in **full sun**, **partial shade** or **light shade**. Grow them in **fertile, moist, well-drained** soil that is high in **organic matter**.

Tips

Black-eyed Susan vines can be trained to twine up and around fences, walls, trees and shrubs. They are also attractive trailing down from the top of a rock garden or rock wall or growing in mixed containers and hanging baskets.

Recommended

T. alata is a vigorous, twining climber. It bears yellow flowers, often with dark centers, in summer and fall. Cultivars with large flowers in yellow, orange or white are available.

T. grandiflora (skyflower vine, blue trumpet vine) is less commonly available than *T. alata*. It tends to bloom late, in early to mid-fall. This twining climber bears stunning, pale violet-blue flowers. **'Alba'** has white flowers.

T. alata (above & below)

The blooms are actually trumpet-shaped, with the dark centers forming a tube.

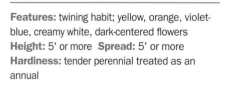

Features: twining habit; yellow, orange, violet-blue, creamy white, dark-centered flowers
Height: 5' or more **Spread:** 5' or more
Hardiness: tender perennial treated as an annual

Clematis

Clematis

C. 'Etoile Violette' (above), C. 'Gravetye Beauty' (below)

There are so many species, hybrids and cultivars of clematis that it is possible to have one in bloom all season.

Growing

Clematis plants prefer **full sun** but tolerate partial shade. The soil should be **fertile, humus rich, moist** and **well drained**. These vines enjoy warm, sunny weather, but the roots prefer to be cool. A thick layer of mulch or a planting of low, shade-providing perennials will protect the tender roots. Clematis are quite cold hardy but will fare best when protected from winter wind. The rootball of vining clematis should be planted about 2" beneath the surface of the soil.

Tips

Clematis vines can climb up structures such as trellises, railings, fences and arbors. They can also be allowed to grow over shrubs and up trees and can be used as groundcover.

Recommended

There are many species, hybrids and cultivars of clematis. The flower forms, blooming times and sizes of the plants can vary. Check with your local garden center to see what is available.

Features: twining habit; blue, purple, pink, yellow, red, white, early-to late-summer flowers; decorative seedheads **Height:** 10–17' or more **Spread:** 5' or more **Hardiness:** zones 3–8

Climbing Hydrangea

Hydrangea

H. anomala subsp. *petiolaris* (above & below)

A mature climbing hydrangea can cover an entire wall, and with its dark, glossy leaves and delicate, lacy flowers, it is quite possibly one of the most stunning climbing plants available.

Growing

Hydrangeas prefer **partial or light shade** but tolerate full sun or full shade. The soil should be of **average to high fertility, humus rich, moist** and **well drained**. These plants perform best in cool, moist conditions, so be sure to mulch their roots.

Tips

Climbing hydrangea climbs up trees, walls, fences, pergolas and arbors. It clings to walls by means of aerial roots so needs no support, just a somewhat textured surface. It also grows over rocks, can be used as a groundcover and can be trained to form a small tree or shrub.

Recommended

H. anomala subsp. *petiolaris* (*H. petiolaris*) is a clinging vine with dark, glossy green leaves that sometimes turn an attractive yellow in fall. For more than a month in mid-summer, the vine is covered with white, lacy-looking flowers, and the entire plant appears to be veiled in a lacy mist.

Climbing hydrangea will produce the most flowers when it is exposed to some direct sunlight each day.

Features: white flowers; clinging habit; exfoliating bark **Height:** 50–80'
Spread: 50–80' **Hardiness:** zones 4–9

Cup-and-Saucer Vine
Cobaea

Cup-and-saucer vine is a vigorous climber native to Mexico that produces frilly, purple flowers from spring until frost.

Growing
Cup-and-saucer vine prefers **full sun**. The soil should be **well drained** and of **average fertility**. This plant is fond of hot weather and will do best if planted in a sheltered site with southern exposure. Set the seeds on edge when planting them and barely cover them with soil.

Tips
Grow this vine up a trellis, over an arbor or along a chain-link fence. Cup-and-saucer vine requires a sturdy support in order to climb. It uses grabbing hooks to climb so won't be able to grow up a wall without something to grab. It can be trained to fill almost any space. In hanging baskets the vines will climb the hanger and spill over the edges.

C. scandens (above & below)

These tender plants can be cut back a bit in fall and overwintered indoors. Plants grown in hanging baskets are the easiest to move indoors.

Recommended
C. scandens is a vigorous climbing vine with flowers that are creamy green when they open and mature to deep purple. **Var.** *alba* has white flowers.

Also called: cathedral bells **Features:** purple or white flowers; clinging habit; long blooming period **Height:** 15–25' **Spread:** 15–25' **Hardiness:** tender perennial; treated as an annual

Hardy Kiwi
Actinidia

Hardy kiwi is handsome in its simplicity, and its lush green leaves, vigor and adaptability make it very useful, especially on difficult sites.

Growing

Hardy kiwi vines grow best in **full sun**. The soil should be **fertile** and **well drained**. These plants require shelter from strong winds.

Tips

These vines need a sturdy structure to twine around. Pergolas, arbors and sufficiently large and sturdy fences provide good support. Given a trellis against a wall, a tree or some other upright structure, hardy kiwis will twine upward all summer. They can also be grown in containers.

Hardy kiwi vines can grow uncontrollably. Don't be afraid to prune them back if they are getting out of hand.

Recommended

There are two hardy kiwi vines commonly grown in Pennsylvania gardens. *A. arguta* (hardy kiwi, bower actinidia) has dark green, heart-shaped leaves, white flowers and smooth-skinned, greenish yellow, edible fruit. *A. kolomikta* (variegated kiwi vine, kolomikta actinidia) has green leaves strongly variegated with pink and white, white flowers and smooth-skinned, greenish yellow, edible fruit.

A. kolomikta (above)

Both a male and a female vine must be present for fruit to be produced. The plants are often sold in pairs.

Features: white, early-summer flowers; edible fruit; twining habit **Height:** 15–30' to indefinite **Spread:** 15–30' to indefinite **Hardiness:** zones 3–8

Honeysuckle
Lonicera

Honeysuckles can be rampant twining vines, but with careful consideration and placement they won't overrun your garden. The fragrance of the flowers makes any effort worthwhile.

Growing
Honeysuckles grow well in **full sun** or **partial shade**. The soil should be **average to fertile, humus rich, moist** and **well drained**.

Tips
Honeysuckle can be trained to grow up a trellis, fence, arbor or other structure. In a large container near a porch it will ramble over the edges of the pot and up the railings with reckless abandon.

Recommended
There are dozens of honeysuckle species, hybrids and cultivars. Check with your local garden center to see what is available. The following are two popular species.

L. sempervirens (trumpet honeysuckle, coral honeysuckle) bears orange or red flowers in late spring and early summer. Many cultivars and hybrids are available with flowers in yellow, red or scarlet, including *L.* x *brownii* 'Dropmore Scarlet,' one of the hardiest of the climbing honeysuckles, cold hardy to zone 4. It bears bright red flowers for most of the summer.

L. caprifolium (Italian honeysuckle, Italian woodbine) bears fragrant, creamy white or yellow flowers in late spring and early summer.

L. x *brownii* 'Dropmore Scarlet' (above & below)

Features: yellow, red, scarlet, white, yellow late spring and early-summer flowers; twining habit; fruit **Height:** 6–20' **Spread:** 6–20' **Hardiness:** zones 5–8

Japanese Hydrangea Vine

Schizophragma

This vine is similar in appearance to climbing hydrangea, but has a few interesting cultivars to add variety.

Growing

Japanese hydrangea vine grows well in **full sun** or **partial shade**. The soil should be **average to fertile, humus rich, moist** and **well drained**.

This vine will have trouble clinging to a smooth-surfaced wall. Attach a few supports to the wall and tie the vines to these. The dense growth will eventually hide the support.

Tips

This vine will cling to any rough surface and looks attractive climbing a wall, fence, tree, pergola or arbor. It can also be used as a groundcover on a bank or allowed to grow up or over a rock wall.

Recommended

S. hydrangeoides is an attractive climbing vine similar in appearance to climbing hydrangea. It bears lacy clusters of white flowers in midsummer. **'Moonlight'** has silvery blue foliage. **'Roseum'** bears clusters of pink flowers.

This elegant vine adds a touch of glamour to even the most ordinary-looking home.

S. hydrangeoides (above & below)

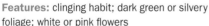

Features: clinging habit; dark green or silvery foliage; white or pink flowers
Height: up to 40' **Spread:** up to 40'
Hardiness: zones 5–8

Morning Glory
Ipomoea

I. tricolor (above & below)

The brightly colored flowers of morning glory are produced in abundance, giving even the dullest fence or wall a splash of excitement.

Growing

Morning glory grows best in **full sun**. The soil should be of **poor to average fertility, light** and **well drained**, though these plants adapt to most soil conditions. These plants twine around narrow objects to climb and must be provided with a trellis or wires if grown against a fence with broad boards, a wall or other surface they won't be able to wind around.

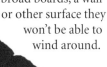

Tips

These vines can be grown on fences, walls, trees, trellises and arbors. As groundcovers, morning glories will grow over any objects they encounter. They can also be grown in hanging baskets or containers where they will spill over the edges.

Recommended

I. purpurea is a twining climber that bears trumpet-shaped flowers in shades of purple, blue, pink or white. Cultivars are available.

I. tricolor is a twining climber that bears trumpet-shaped flowers in shades of blue and purple, often with lighter or white centers. Many cultivars are available, including '**Heavenly Blue**' with white-centered, sky-blue flowers.

Features: fast-growing twining habit; purple, blue, pink, white flowers; foliage **Height:** 6–12' **Spread:** 6–12' **Hardiness:** tender annual

Passion Flower

Passiflora

Exotic and mesmerizing, passion flowers are sure to attract attention in your garden.

Growing

Passion flower grows well in **full sun** or **partial shade** in a location sheltered from wind and cold. The soil should be of **average fertility, moist** and **well drained**.

Tips

Passion flower is a popular addition to mixed containers and creates an unusual focal point near a door or other entryway. Provided with a trellis or other structure, it will quickly climb all summer, though not as much as some of the other annual vines.

Recommended

P. caerulea is a vigorous, woody climber with deeply lobed leaves. It bears unusual purple-banded, purple-white flowers all summer. It can grow up to 30' tall, but usually only grows 5–10' over the course of the summer. Hardy to zone 6, it may survive the winter in some Pennsylvania gardens.

P. caerulea (above & below)

Passion flowers can be composted at the end of the season, or cut back and either brought indoors for the winter where they aren't hardy or left in a sheltered location outdoors where they are.

Features: exotic purple-white flowers; attractive foliage **Height:** 5–10' **Spread:** variable **Hardiness:** zones 6–9; often grown as an annual

Sweet Pea
Lathyrus

L. odoratus (above & below)

Newer sweet pea cultivars often have less fragrant flowers than old-fashioned cultivars. Look for heritage varieties to enjoy the most fragrant flowers.

Sweet peas are among the most enchanting annuals. Their fragrance is intoxicating, and the flowers in double tones and shimmering shades look like no other annual in the garden.

Growing
Sweet peas prefer **full sun** but tolerate light shade. The soil should be **fertile,** high in **organic matter, moist** and **well drained**. The plants tolerate light frost.

Soak seeds in water for 24 hours or nick them with a nail file before planting them. Planting a second crop of sweet peas about a month after the first one will ensure a longer blooming period. Deadhead all spent blooms.

Tips
Sweet peas will grow up poles, trellises, fences or over rocks. They cling by wrapping tendrils around whatever they are growing up, so they do best when they have a rough surface, chain-link fence, small twigs or a net to cling to.

Recommended
There are many cultivars of **L. odoratus** available, though many are now small and bushy rather than climbing. **'Bouquet'** is a tall, climbing variety with flowers in a wide range of colors.

Features: clinging habit; pink, red, purple, lavender, blue, salmon, pale yellow, peach, white, bicolored summer flowers **Height:** 1–6' **Spread:** 6–12" **Hardiness:** hardy annual

Virginia Creeper • Boston Ivy

Parthenocissus

P. quinquefolia (above & below)

Virginia creeper and Boston ivy are handsome vines that establish quickly and provide an air of age and permanence, even on new structures.

Growing

These vines grow well in any light, from **full sun to full shade**. The soil should be **fertile** and **well drained**. The plants will adapt to clay or sandy soils.

Tips

Virginia creepers can cover an entire building, given enough time. They do not require support because they have clinging rootlets that adhere to just about any surface, even smooth wood, vinyl or metal. Give the plants a lot of space and let them cover a wall, fence or arbor.

Recommended

These two species are very similar, except for the shape of the leaves.

P. quinquefolia (Virginia creeper, woodbine) has dark green foliage. Each leaf, divided into five leaflets, turns flame red in fall.

P. tricuspidata (Boston ivy, Japanese creeper) has dark green, three-lobed leaves that turn red in fall. This species is not quite as hardy as Virginia creeper. (Zones 4–8)

Features: summer and fall foliage; clinging habit **Height:** 30–70' **Spread:** 30–70' **Hardiness:** zones 3–9

Canna Lily
Canna

*C*anna lilies are stunning, dramatic plants that give an exotic flair to any garden.

Growing

Canna lilies grow best in **full sun** in a **sheltered** location. The soil should be **fertile, moist** and **well drained**. Plant out in spring, once soil has warmed. Plants can be started early indoors in containers to get a head start on the growing season. Deadhead to prolong blooming.

Tips

Canna lilies can be grown in a bed or border. They make dramatic specimen plants and can even be included in large planters.

Recommended

A wide range of canna lilies are available, including cultivars and hybrids with green, bronzy, purple or yellow-and-green-striped foliage. Flowers may be white, red, orange, pink, yellow or bicolored. Dwarf cultivars that grow 18–28" tall are also available.

C. 'Red King Humbert' (above & below)

The rhizomes can be lifted after the foliage is killed back in fall. Clean off any clinging dirt and store them in a cool, frost-free location in slightly moist peat moss. Check on them regularly through the winter and if they are starting to sprout, pot them and move them to a bright window until they can be moved outdoors.

Features: decorative foliage; white, red, orange, pink, yellow, bicolored summer flowers
Height: 3–6' **Spread:** 20–36"
Hardiness: zones 7–9; grown as an annual

Crocus

Crocus

C. x *vernus* cultivars (above & below)

Crocuses are harbingers of spring. They often appear, as if by magic, in full bloom from beneath the melting snow.

Growing

Crocuses grow well in **full sun** or **light, dappled shade**. The soil should be of **poor to average fertility, gritty** and **well drained**. The corms are planted about 4" deep in fall.

Tips

Crocuses are almost always planted in groups. Drifts of crocuses can be planted in lawns to provide interest and color while the grass still lies dormant. In beds and borders they can be left to naturalize. The plants will fill in and spread out, giving a bright welcome in spring.

Recommended

Many crocus species, hybrids and cultivars are available. The spring-flowering crocus most people are familiar with is **C. x *vernus*,** commonly called Dutch crocus. Many cultivars are available with flowers in shades of purple, yellow or white, sometimes bicolored or with darker veins.

Features: purple, yellow, white, bicolored early-spring flowers **Height:** 2–6"
Spread: 2–4" **Hardiness:** zones 3–8

Daffodil
Narcissus

Many gardeners automatically think of large, yellow, trumpet-shaped flowers when they think of daffodils, but there is plenty of variation in color, form and size among the daffodils.

Growing

Daffodils grow best in **full sun** or **light, dappled shade**. The soil should be **average to fertile, moist** and **well drained**. Bulbs should be planted in fall, 2–8" deep, depending on the size of the bulb. The bigger the bulb the deeper it should be planted. A rule of thumb is to measure the bulb from top to bottom and multiply that number by three to know how deeply to plant.

Tips

Daffodils are often planted where they can be left to naturalize, in the light shade beneath a tree or in a woodland garden. In mixed beds and borders, the faded leaves are hidden by the summer foliage of other plants.

Recommended

Many species, hybrids and cultivars of daffodils are available. Flowers come in shades of white, yellow, peach, orange or pink, and may also be bicolored. Flowers range from 1¹/₂–6" across, and can be solitary or borne in clusters. There are about 12 flower form categories.

Features: white, yellow, peach, orange, pink, bicolored spring flowers **Height:** 4–24"
Spread: 4–12" **Hardiness:** zones 3–9

Dahlia

Dahlia

*T*he variation in size, shape and color of dahlia flowers is astonishing. You are sure to find at least one that appeals to you.

Growing

Dahlias prefer **full sun**. The soil should be **fertile,** rich in **organic matter, moist** and **well drained**. All dahlias are tender, tuberous perennials treated as annuals. Tubers can be purchased and started early indoors. The tubers can also be lifted in fall and stored over winter in slightly moist peat moss. Pot them and keep them in a bright room when they start sprouting in mid- to late winter. Deadhead to keep plants tidy and blooming.

Tips

Dahlias make attractive, colorful additions to a mixed border. The smaller varieties make good edging plants, and the larger ones make good alternatives to shrubs. Varieties with unusual or interesting flowers are attractive specimen plants.

Recommended

Of the many dahlia hybrids, most are purchased as and grown from tubers but a few can be started from seed. Many hybrids are sold based on flower shape, such as collarette, decorative or peony-flowered. The flowers range in size from 2–12" and are available in shades of purple, pink, white, yellow, orange or red with some bicolored. Check with your local garden center to see what is available.

Dahlia cultivars span a vast array of colors, sizes and flower forms, but breeders have yet to develop true blue, scented or frost-hardy selections.

Features: purple, pink, white, yellow, orange, red, bicolored summer flowers; attractive foliage; bushy habit **Height:** 8"–5'
Spread: 8–18" **Hardiness:** tender perennials; grown as annuals

Flowering Onion
Allium

A. giganteum (above), A. cernuum (below)

Although the leaves have an onion scent when bruised, the flowers are often sweetly fragrant.

Flowering onions, with their striking, ball-like to loose, nodding clusters of flowers, are sure to attract attention in the garden.

Growing
Flowering onions grow best in **full sun**. The soil should be **average to fertile, moist** and **well drained**. Plant bulbs in fall, 2–4" deep, depending on size of bulb.

Tips
Flowering onions are best planted in groups in a bed or border where they can be left to naturalize. Most will self-seed when left to their own devices. The foliage, which tends to fade just as the plants come into flower, can be hidden with groundcover or a low, bushy companion plant.

Recommended
Several flowering onion species, hybrids and cultivars have gained popularity for their decorative pink, purple, white, yellow, blue or maroon flowers. These include *A. aflatunense*, with dense, globe-like clusters of lavender flowers; *A. caeruleum* (blue globe onion), with globe-like clusters of blue flowers; *A. cernuum* (nodding or wild onion), with loose, drooping clusters of pink flowers; and *A. giganteum* (giant onion), a big plant that grows up to 6' tall, with large, globe-shaped clusters of pinky purple flowers.

Features: pink, purple, white, yellow, blue, maroon summer flowers; cylindrical or strap-shaped leaves **Height:** 1–6' **Spread:** 2–12" **Hardiness:** zones 3–9

Gladiolus

Gladiolus

Perhaps best known as a cut flower, gladiolus adds an air of extravagance to the garden.

Growing

Gladiolus grows best in **full sun** but tolerates partial shade. The soil should be **fertile, humus rich, moist** and **well drained**. Flower spikes may need staking and a sheltered location out of the wind to prevent the flower spike from blowing over.

Plant corms in spring, 4–6" deep, once soil has warmed. Corms can also be started early indoors. Plant a few corms each week for about a month to prolong the blooming period.

Tips

Planted in groups in beds and borders, gladiolus makes a bold statement. Corms can also be pulled up in fall and stored in damp peat moss in a cool, frost-free location for the winter.

Recommended

G. x *hortulanus* is a huge group of hybrids. Gladiolus flowers come in almost every imaginable shade, except blue. Plants are commonly grouped in three classifications: **grandiflorus** is the best known, each corm producing a single spike of large, often ruffled flowers; **nanus**, the hardiest group, can survive in zone 3 with protection and produces several spikes of up to seven flowers; and **primulinus** produces a single spike of up to 23 flowers that are more spaced out on the spike than those of grandiflorus.

Over 10,000 cultivars of gladiolus have been developed.

Features: brightly colored mid- to late-summer flowers **Height:** 1¹/₂–6' **Spread:** 6–12"
Hardiness: zones 8–10; grown as an annual

Grape Hyacinth
Muscari

M. armeniacum cultivars (above), *M. botryoides* (below)

It's not difficult to see where these bulbs get their common name. The purple or blue flowers, borne densely clustered on spikes, do indeed look like bunches of grapes.

Growing

Grape hyacinths grow best in **full sun** but tolerate partial or light shade. The soil should be **average to fertile, humus rich, moist** and **well drained**. Plant bulbs 3–4" deep in fall.

Tips

Planted in masses or small groups, grape hyacinths make a great spring accent plant, blending well with other bulbs and spring-blooming plants. They can be left to naturalize in borders and even in lawns, where they create a good excuse for not mowing your lawn in spring.

Recommended

M. armeniacum (Armenian grape hyacinth) forms a low-growing clump of narrow grass-like leaves. The bright blue or purple flowers are densely clustered on spikes. **'Mt. Hood'** has bicolored flower clusters. The upper third are white while the lower flowers are blue. **'Fantasy Creation'** has large, pyramidal, blue flower clusters that resemble heads of broccoli. The flowers of this cultivar fade to yellow and are popular for dried-flower arrangements. **'Valerie Finnis'** bears large spikes of plump, pale blue flowers. Its origin is uncertain and it is sometimes considered a cultivar of *M. neglectum.* (Zones 4–8)

M. botryoides (common grape hyacinth) is similar in appearance to Armenian grape hyacinth, but the plants are much smaller. Flowers are pale blue. **'Album'** has white flowers.

M. comosum **'Plumosum'** has feathery, bright red-violet flowers on the spikes that are plumy rather than grape-like. (Zones 4–8)

Features: blue, white, yellow, purple spring flowers; good for naturalizing **Height:** 4–8" **Spread:** 6–12" **Hardiness:** zones 2–8

Lily
Lilium

ecorative clusters of large, richly colored blooms grace these tall plants. Flowers are produced at differing times of the season, depending on the hybrid, and it is possible to have lilies blooming all season if a variety of cultivars are chosen.

Growing

Lilies grow best in **full sun** but like to have their **roots shaded**. The soil should be rich in **organic matter, fertile, moist** and **well drained**.

Tips

Lilies are often grouped in beds and borders and can be naturalized in woodland gardens and near water features. These plants are narrow but tall; plant at least three plants together to create some volume.

Recommended

The many species, hybrids and cultivars available are grouped by type. Visit your local garden center to see what is available. The following are two popular groups of lilies. **Asiatic Hybrids** bear clusters of flowers in early summer or mid-summer and are available in a wide range of colors. **Oriental Hybrids** bear clusters of large, fragrant flowers in mid- and late summer. Colors are usually white, pink or red.

Asiatic Hybrids (above), 'Stargazer' (below)

Lily bulbs should be planted in fall before the first frost, but they can also be planted in spring if bulbs are available.

Features: early, mid- or late-season flowers in shades of orange, yellow, peach, pink, purple, red, white **Height:** 2–5' **Spread:** 12"
Hardiness: zones 4–8

Snowdrops
Galanthus

G. *elwesii* with winter aconite (above), G. *nivalis* (below)

These are the first bulbs to bloom, often as early as January. Their delicate, white nodding flowers pierce through the snow, giving us a taste of a still distant spring.

Growing

Snowdrops prefer to grow in **partial or light shade** but happily tolerate all light conditions from full sun to full shade. The soil should be of **average fertility, humus rich, moist** and **well drained**.

Snowdrops prefer not to have their soil dry out completely in summer. Plant bulbs 4" deep and 2" apart. Divide or move plants as soon as possible after flowering is complete in spring.

Tips

Snowdrops are popular bulbs for naturalizing. They can be planted in mixed beds and borders, thriving at the feet of deciduous shrubs and in meadow plantings.

Recommended

G. elwesii (giant snowdrop) forms a clump of bright green, strap-shaped leaves. It bears fragrant, white flowers in late winter. It grows 5–12" tall.

G. nivalis (common snowdrop) forms a clump of long, narrow leaves. It bears small, white, fragrant flowers in winter and grows about 4" tall. **'Flore Pleno'** bears double flowers.

Features: white, early-spring flowers **Height:** 4–12" **Spread:** 2–6" **Hardiness:** zones 3–9

Spring Starflower
Ipheion

I. uniflorum 'Wisely Blue'

*L*ovely, fragrant, single star-shaped flowers of blue, white or lavender form clusters in late winter and early to mid-spring.

Growing
Spring starflowers grow well in **full sun** or **partial shade**. The soil should be of **average fertility, humus rich, moist** and **well drained**. Plant the bulbs 3–4" deep in fall. Plants can be divided in summer while they are dormant.

Tips
Spring starflowers make an excellent addition to mixed beds and borders where they can be planted to fill in the spaces beneath shrubs and between perennials. They are dormant in summer but provide a welcome show of bright green in fall that lasts through the winter

I. uniflorum

before they flower in spring. They can also be included in containers and rock gardens.

Recommended
I. uniflorum forms a clump of narrow, strap-shaped leaves. Clumps can spread quickly. Fragrant, silvery blue flowers are borne in spring. Several cultivars are available with flowers in different colors. **'Alba'** bears white flowers. **'Froyle Mill'** bears lavender flowers. **'Rolf Feidler'** bears blue flowers with rounded petals and spreads more slowly than the species and other cultivars. **'Wisley Blue'** bears pale blue flowers.

Features: blue, white, lavender spring flowers; fall and winter foliage **Height:** 6–8" **Spread:** 4–8" **Hardiness:** zones 5–9

Spring starflowers send up fresh, green, onion-scented leaves in fall that remain throughout winter. Deer don't eat them.

Tulip
Tulipa

ulips, with their beautiful, often garishly colored flowers, are a welcome sight as we enjoy the warm days of spring.

Growing

Tulips grow best in **full sun**. If they are placed in light or partial shade, the flowers will bend toward the light. The soil should be **fertile** and **well drained**. Plant bulbs in fall, 4–6" deep, depending on size of bulb. Bulbs that have been cold treated can be planted in spring. Although tulips can repeat bloom, many hybrids perform best if planted new each year. Species and older cultivars are the best choice for naturalizing.

Tips

Tulips provide the best display when mass planted or planted in groups in flowerbeds and borders. They can also be grown in containers and can be forced to bloom early in pots indoors. Some of the species and older cultivars can be naturalized in meadow and wildflower gardens.

Recommended

There are about 100 species of tulips and thousands of hybrids and cultivars. They are generally divided into 15 groups based on bloom time and flower appearance. They come in dozens of shades, with many bicolored or multi-colored varieties. Blue is the only shade not available. Check with your local garden center in early fall for the best selection.

Features: spring flowers **Height:** 6–30"
Spread: 2–8" **Hardiness:** zones 3–8; often treated as annuals

Basil
Ocimum

The sweet, fragrant leaves of fresh basil add a delicious, licorice-like flavor to salads and tomato-based dishes.

Growing
Basil grows best in a **warm, sheltered** location in **full sun**. The soil should be **fertile, moist** and **well drained**. Pinch the tips regularly to encourage bushy growth. Plant out or direct sow seed after frost danger has passed in spring.

Tips
Although basil will grow best in a warm spot outdoors in the garden, it can be grown successfully in a pot by a bright window indoors to provide you with fresh leaves all year.

Recommended
O. basilicum is one of the most popular of the culinary herbs. There are dozens of varieties including ones with large or tiny, green or purple and smooth or ruffled leaves.

O. basilicum 'Genovese' (above & below)

O. x citriodorum (lemon basil) is a deliciously lemon-scented and flavored basil for soups, salads, fish, potato and tomato dishes.

Basil is a good companion plant for tomatoes—both like warm, moist growing conditions, and when you pick tomatoes for a salad you'll also remember to include a few sprigs or leaves of basil.

Features: fragrant, decorative leaves
Height: 12–24" **Spread:** 12–18"
Hardiness: tender annual

Chives

Allium

A. schoenoprasum (above & below)

Chives are said to increase appetite and encourage good digestion.

The delicate onion flavor of chives is best enjoyed fresh. Mix chives into dips or sprinkle them on salads and baked potatoes.

Growing

Chives grow best in **full sun**. The soil should be **fertile, moist** and **well drained**, but chives adapt to most soil conditions. These plants are easy to start from seed, but they do like the soil temperature to stay above 65°F before they will germinate, so seeds started directly in the garden are unlikely to sprout before early summer.

Tips

Chives are decorative enough to be included in a mixed or herbaceous border and can be left to naturalize. In an herb garden, chives should be given plenty of space to allow self-seeding.

Recommended

A. schoenoprasum forms a clump of bright green, cylindrical leaves. Clusters of pinky purple flowers are produced in early and mid-summer. Varieties with white or pink flowers are available.

Be cautious when growing *A. tuberosum* (garlic chives), however. Beautiful and useful as they are with their white flowers blooming late in summer, if you let them go to seed, they will likely be everywhere in your garden, as they are far more aggressive self-seeders than ordinary chives.

Features: foliage; form; white, pink flowers
Height: 8–24" **Spread:** 12" or more
Hardiness: zones 3–9

Coriander • Cilantro

Coriandrum

Coriander is a multi-purpose herb. The leaves, called cilantro and used in salads, salsas and soups; the seeds, called coriander and used in pies, chutneys and marmalades, have distinct flavors and culinary uses.

Growing

Coriander prefers **full sun** but tolerates partial shade. The soil should be **fertile, light** and **well drained**. These plants dislike humid conditions and do best during a dry summer.

Tips

Coriander has pungent leaves and is best planted where people will not have to brush past it. It is, however, a delight to behold when in flower.

Add a plant or two here and there throughout your borders and vegetable garden, both for the visual appeal and to attract beneficial insects.

Recommended

C. sativum forms a clump of lacy basal foliage above which large, loose clusters of tiny, white flowers are produced. The seeds ripen in late summer and fall.

The flowers of this herb attract bees and butterflies, as well as predatory insects that help control garden pests.

C. sativum (above & below)

Features: form; foliage; white flowers; seeds
Height: 18–24" **Spread:** 8–18"
Hardiness: tender annual

Dill
Anethum

A. graveolens (above & below)

Dill leaves and seeds are probably best known for their use as pickling herbs, though they have a wide variety of other culinary uses.

Growing
Dill grows best in **full sun** in a **sheltered** location out of strong winds. The soil should be of **poor to average fertility, moist** and **well drained**. Sow seeds every couple of weeks in spring and early summer to ensure a regular supply of leaves.

Plants should not be grown near fennel because they will cross-pollinate and the seeds of both plants will lose their distinct flavors.

Tips
With its feathery leaves, dill is an attractive addition to a mixed bed or border. It can be included in a vegetable garden but does well in any sunny location. It also attracts predatory insects to the garden.

Recommended
A. graveolens forms a clump of feathery foliage. Clusters of yellow flowers are borne at the tops of sturdy stems.

Dill turns up frequently in historical records as both a culinary and medicinal herb. It was used by the Egyptians and Romans and is mentioned in the Bible.

A popular Scandinavian dish called gravalax is made by marinating a fillet of salmon with the leaves and seeds of dill.

Features: feathery, edible foliage; yellow summer flowers; edible seeds **Height:** 2–5' **Spread:** 12" or more **Hardiness:** annual

Fennel
Foeniculum

*A*ll parts of fennel are edible and have a distinctive licorice-like fragrance and flavor. The seeds are commonly used to make a tea, which is good for settling the stomach after a large meal.

Growing
Fennel grows best in **full sun**. The soil should be **average to fertile**, **moist** and **well drained**. Avoid planting near dill and coriander as cross pollination reduces seed production and the seed flavor of each becomes less distinct. Fennel will easily self-sow in the garden.

Tips
Fennel is an attractive addition to a mixed bed or border. It can be included in a vegetable garden but does well in any sunny location. It also attracts pollinators and predatory insects to the garden. To collect seeds, remove the seed-bearing stems before the seeds start to fall off.

Recommended
F. vulgare is a short-lived perennial that forms clumps of loose, feathery foliage. Clusters of small yellow flowers are borne in late summer; seeds ripen in fall. A large, edible bulb forms at the stem base of the biennial **var. azoricum**. The bulb is popular raw in salads, cooked in soups and stews and roasted like other root vegetables. **'Purpureum'** is similar in appearance to the species but has bronzy purple foliage.

F. vulgare (above), F. vulgare 'Purpureum' (below)

Fennel has been used for its medicinal and culinary properties since before ancient Greek times.

Features: attractive, fragrant foliage; yellow flowers; seeds; stems **Height:** 2–6'
Spread: 12–24" **Hardiness:** zones 4–9

Mint

Mentha

M. x *piperata* with Lemon Balm (above)
M. x gracilis 'Variegata' (decorative cultivar; below)

*A few sprigs of fresh
mint added to a pitcher
of iced tea gives it an
added zip.*

𝒯he cool, refreshing flavor of mint lends itself to tea and other hot or cold beverages. Mint sauce, made from freshly chopped leaves, is often served with lamb.

Growing

Mint grows well in **full sun** or **partial shade**. The soil should be **average to fertile, humus rich** and **moist**. These plants spread vigorously by rhizomes and may need a barrier in the soil to restrict their spread.

Tips

Mint is a good groundcover for damp spots. It grows well along ditches that may only be periodically wet. It also can be used in beds and borders but may overwhelm less vigorous plants.

The flowers attract bees, butterflies and other pollinators to the garden.

Recommended

There are many species, hybrids and cultivars of mint. Spearmint (**M. spicata**), peppermint (**M.** x **piperita**) and orange mint (**M.** x **piperata citrata**) are three of the most commonly grown culinary varieties. There are also more decorative varieties with variegated or curly leaves as well as varieties with unusual, fruit-scented leaves.

Features: fragrant foliage; purple, pink, white summer flowers **Height:** 6–36" **Spread:** 36" or more **Hardiness:** zones 4–8

Oregano • Marjoram

Origanum

Oregano and marjoram are two of the best known and most frequently used herbs. They are popular in stuffings, soups and stews, and no pizza is complete until it has been sprinkled with fresh or dried oregano leaves.

Growing

Oregano and marjoram grow best in **full sun**. The soil should be of **poor to average fertility, neutral to alkaline** and **well drained**. The flowers attract pollinators to the garden.

Tips

These bushy perennials make a lovely addition to any border and can be trimmed to form low hedges.

Recommended

O. majorana (marjoram) is upright and shrubby with light green, hairy leaves. It bears white or pink flowers in summer and can be grown as an annual where it is not hardy.

O. vulgare var. *hirtum* (oregano, Greek oregano) is the most flavorful culinary variety of oregano. The low, bushy plant has hairy, gray-green leaves and bears white flowers. Many other interesting varieties of *O. vulgare* are available, including those with golden, variegated or curly leaves.

O. vulgare 'Aureum' (above & below)

In Greek, oros *means 'mountain' and* ganos *means 'joy and beauty,' so oregano translates as 'joy or beauty of the mountain.'*

Features: fragrant foliage; white or pink summer flowers; bushy habit **Height:** 12–32"
Spread: 8–18" **Hardiness:** zones 5–9

Parsley
Petroselinum

P. crispum (above), P. crispum var. crispum (below)

*A*lthough usually used as a garnish, parsley is rich in vitamins and minerals and is reputed to freshen the breath after garlic- or onion-rich foods are eaten.

Growing
Parsley grows well in **full sun** or **partial shade**. The soil should be of **average to rich fertility, humus rich, moist** and **well drained**. Direct sow seeds because the plants resent transplanting. If you start seeds early, use peat pots so the plants can be potted or planted out without disruption.

Tips
Parsley should be started where you mean to grow it as it doesn't transplant well. Containers of parsley can be kept close to the house for easy picking. The bright green leaves and compact growth habit make parsley a good edging plant for beds and borders.

Recommended
P. crispum forms a clump of bright green, divided leaves. This plant is biennial but is usually grown as an annual because it is the leaves that are desired and not the flowers or seeds. Cultivars may have flat or curly leaves. Flat leaves are more flavorful and curly leaves are more decorative. Dwarf cultivars are also available.

Parsley leaves make a tasty and nutritious addition to salads. Tear freshly picked leaves and sprinkle them over or mix them in your mixed greens.

Features: attractive foliage **Height:** 8–24"
Spread: 12–24" **Hardiness:** zones 5–8; grown as an annual

Rosemary
Rosmarinus

The needle-like leaves of rosemary are used to flavor a wide variety of culinary dishes, including chicken, pork, lamb, rice, tomato and egg dishes.

Growing
Rosemary prefers **full sun** but tolerates partial shade. The soil should be of **poor to average fertility** and **well drained**. These tender shrubs must be moved indoors for the winter.

Tips
Rosemary is often grown in a shrub border where hardy. In Pennsylvania, where it is not hardy, it is usually grown in a container as a specimen or with other plants. Low-growing, spreading plants can be included in a rock garden or along the top of a retaining wall or can be grown in hanging baskets.

Recommended
R. officinalis is a dense, bushy evergreen shrub with narrow, dark green leaves. The habit varies somewhat between cultivars from strongly upright to prostrate and spreading. Flowers are usually in shades of blue, but pink-flowered cultivars are available. Cultivars are available that can survive in zone 6 in a sheltered location with winter protection. Plants rarely reach their mature size when grown in containers.

R. officinalis 'Prostratus' (above), R. officinalis (below)

To overwinter a container-grown plant, keep it in very light or partial shade outdoors in summer, then put it in a sunny window indoors for winter and keep it well watered, but allow it to dry out slightly between waterings.

Features: fragrant, evergreen foliage; bright blue, sometimes pink, summer flowers
Height: 8"–4' **Spread:** 2–4'
Hardiness: zones 8–10

Sage
Salvia

'Icterina' (above), 'Purpurea' (below)

Sage has been used since at least ancient Greek times as a medicinal and culinary herb and continues to be widely used for both those purposes today.

Sage is perhaps best known as a flavoring for stuffings, but it has a great range of uses, including in soups, stews, sausages and dumplings.

Growing

Sage prefers **full sun** but tolerates light shade. The soil should be of **average fertility** and **well drained**. These plants benefit from a light mulch of compost each year. They are drought tolerant once established.

Tips

Sage is an attractive plant for the border, adding volume to the middle of the border or as an attractive edging or feature plant near the front. Sage can also be grown in mixed planters.

Recommended

S. officinalis is a woody, mounding plant with soft, gray-green leaves. Spikes of light purple flowers appear in early and midsummer. Many cultivars with attractive foliage are available, including the silver-leaved **'Berggarten,'** the yellow-margined **'Icterina,'** the purple-leaved **'Purpurea,'** and the purple, green and cream variegated **'Tricolor,'** which has a pink flush to the new growth.

Features: fragrant, decorative foliage; blue or purple summer flowers **Height:** 12–24"
Spread: 18–36" **Hardiness:** zones 5–8

Thyme
Thymus

*T*hyme is a popular culinary herb used in soups, stews, casseroles and with roasts.

Growing
Thyme prefers **full sun**. The soil should be **neutral to alkaline** and of **poor to average fertility. Good drainage** is essential. It is beneficial to work leaf mold and sharp limestone gravel into the soil to improve structure and drainage.

Tips
Thyme is useful in sunny, dry locations at the front of borders, between or beside paving stones, on rock gardens and rock walls, and in containers.

Once the plants have finished flowering, shear them back by about half to encourage new growth and to prevent the plants from becoming too woody.

Recommended
T. x *citriodorus* (lemon-scented thyme) forms a mound of lemon-scented, dark green foliage. The flowers are pale pink. Cultivars with silver- or gold-margined leaves are available.

T. vulgaris (common thyme) forms a bushy mound of dark green leaves. The flowers may be purple, pink or white. Cultivars with variegated leaves are available.

T. vulgaris (above), T. x citriodorus (below)

These plants are bee magnets when blooming; thyme honey is pleasantly herbal and goes very well with biscuits.

Features: bushy habit; fragrant, decorative foliage; purple, pink, white flowers **Height:** 8–16"
Spread: 8–16" **Hardiness:** zones 4–9

Artemisia

Artemisia

A. *ludoviciana* 'Silver King' (above)
A. *ludoviciana* 'Valerie Finnis' (below)

$\mathcal{M}$ost of the artemisias are valued for their silvery foliage, not their flowers. Silver is the ultimate blending color in the garden, because it enhances every other hue combined with it.

Growing
Artemisias grow best in **full sun**. The soil should be of **low to average fertility** and **well drained**. These plants dislike wet, humid conditions.

When artemisias begin to look straggly, cut them back hard to encourage new growth and to maintain a neater form. Divide them every year or two, when plant clumps appear to be thinning in the centers.

Tips
Use artemisias in rock gardens and borders. Their silvery gray foliage makes them good backdrop plants to use behind brightly colored flowers. They are also useful for filling in spaces between other plants. Smaller forms may be used to create knot gardens. These plants can spread and become invasive in the garden.

Recommended
A. ludoviciana (white sage, silver sage) is an upright, clump-forming plant with silvery white foliage. The species is not grown as often as its cultivars. (Zones 4–8)

A. x **'Powis Castle'** is a compact, mounding, shrubby plant with feathery, silvery gray foliage. This hybrid is reliably hardy to zone 6, but it can also grow in colder regions if planted with winter protection in a sheltered site.

A. schmidtiana (silvermound artemisia) is a low, dense, mound-forming perennial with feathery, hairy, silvery gray foliage. **'Nana'** (dwarf silvermound) is very compact and grows only half the size of the species. (Zones 4–8)

Also called: wormwood, sage
Features: silvery gray, feathery or deeply lobed foliage **Height:** 6"–6' **Spread:** 12–36"
Hardiness: zones 3–8

Coleus

Solenostemon (Coleus)

There is a coleus for everyone. From brash yellows, oranges and reds to deep maroon and rose selections, the colors, textures and variations are almost limitless.

Growing

Coleus prefers to grow in **light or partial shade**, but it tolerates full shade if the shade isn't too dense, or full sun if the plants are watered regularly. The soil should be of **rich to average fertility, humus rich, moist** and **well drained**.

Place the seeds in a refrigerator for one or two days before planting them on the soil surface; the cold temperatures will assist in breaking the seeds' dormancy. They need light to germinate. Seedlings will be green at first, but leaf variegation will develop as the plants mature.

Tips

The bold, colorful foliage makes coleus dramatic when the plants are grouped together as edging plants or in beds, borders or mixed containers. Coleus can also be grown indoors as a houseplant in a bright room.

When flower buds develop, it is best to pinch them off, because the plants tend to stretch out and become less attractive after they flower.

Recommended

S. scutellarioides (*Coleus blumei* var. *verschaffeltii*) forms a bushy mound of foliage. The leaf edges range from slightly

Wizard Series (above)

toothed to very ruffled. The leaves are usually multi-colored with shades ranging from pale greenish yellow to deep purple-black. Dozens of cultivars are available, but many cannot be started from seed.

Features: brightly colored foliage; light purple flowers **Height:** 6–36" **Spread:** usually equal to height **Hardiness:** tender perennial; grown as an annual

Dead Nettle
Lamium

L. maculatum 'Lime Light' (above), *L. maculatum* 'Beacon Silver' (below)

These attractive plants, with their striped, dotted or banded silver and green foliage, hug the ground and thrive on only the barest necessities of life.

Growing

Dead nettles prefer **partial to light shade**. They tolerate full sun but may become leggy. The soil should be of **average fertility, humus rich, moist** and **well drained**. The more fertile the soil, the more vigorously the plants will grow. These plants are drought tolerant when grown in the shade but can develop bare patches if the soil is allowed to dry out for extended periods. Divide and replant it in autumn if bare spots become unsightly. Dead nettles remain more compact if sheared back after flowering. If they remain green over winter, shear them back in early spring.

Tips

These plants make useful groundcovers for woodland or shade gardens. Dead nettles also work well under shrubs in a border, where they will help keep weeds down. These plants can spread and become invasive in the garden.

Recommended

L. galeobdolon (*Lamiastrum galeobdolon*; yellow archangel) can be quite invasive, though the cultivars are less so. The flowers are yellow and bloom in spring to early summer. Several cultivars are available.

L. maculatum (spotted dead nettle) is the most commonly grown dead nettle. This low-growing, spreading species has green leaves with white or silvery markings and bears white, pink or mauve flowers. Many cultivars are available.

Also called: spotted dead nettle, lamium, yellow archangel **Features:** spring or summer flowers in white, pink, yellow, mauve; decorative, often variegated foliage **Height:** 4–24" **Spread:** indefinite **Hardiness:** zones 3–8

Dusty Miller
Senecio

S. cineraria 'Cirrus' (above), *S. cineraria* (below)

Dusty miller makes an artful addition to planters, window boxes and mixed borders where the soft, silvery gray, deeply lobed foliage makes a good backdrop to show off the brightly colored flowers of other annuals.

Growing
Dusty miller prefers **full sun** but tolerates light shade. The soil should be of **average fertility** and **well drained**.

Tips
The soft, silvery, lacy leaves of this plant is its main feature. Dusty miller is used primarily as an edging plant but also in beds, borders and containers.

Features: silvery foliage; neat habit
Height: 12–24" **Spread:** equal to height or slightly narrower **Hardiness:** tender perennial; grown as an annual

Pinch off the flowers before they bloom. They aren't showy and they steal energy that would otherwise go to producing more foliage.

Recommended
S. cineraria forms a mound of fuzzy, silvery gray, lobed or finely divided foliage. Many cultivars have been developed with impressive foliage colors and shapes.

Fescue

Festuca

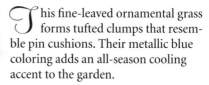

This fine-leaved ornamental grass forms tufted clumps that resemble pin cushions. Their metallic blue coloring adds an all-season cooling accent to the garden.

Growing

Fescue thrives in **full sun to light shade**. The soil should be of **average fertility**, **moist** and **well drained**. These plants are drought tolerant once established. Fescue emerges early in the spring, so shear it back to 1" above the crown in late winter, before new growth emerges. Shear off flower stalks just above the foliage to keep the plant tidy and to prevent self-seeding.

Tips

With its fine texture and distinct blue color, this grass can be used as a single specimen in a rock garden or a container planting. Plant fescue in drifts to create a sea of blue or a handsome edge to a bed, border or pathway. It looks attractive in both formal and informal gardens.

F. glauca 'Elijah Blue' (above), *F. glauca* (below)

If you enjoy blue grass, you might also like the large, coarse-textured blue oat grass, Helicotrichon sempervirens 'Saphirsprudel' (Sapphire Fountain), which can grow 4' tall when in flower.

Recommended

F. glauca (blue fescue) forms tidy, tufted clumps of fine, blue-toned foliage and panicles of flowers in May and June. Cultivars and hybrids come in varying heights and in shades ranging from blue to olive green. **'Elijah Blue,' 'Boulder Blue,' 'Skinner's Blue'** and **'Solling'** are popular selections.

Also called: blue fescue **Features:** blue to blue-green foliage; color that persists into winter; habit **Height:** 6–12" **Spread:** 10–12" **Hardiness:** zones 3–9

Flowering Fern
Osmunda

O. cinnamomea (above), *O. regalis* (below)

Ferns have a prehistoric mystique and can add a graceful elegance and textural accent to the garden.

Growing

Flowering ferns prefer **light shade** but tolerate full sun if the soil is consistently moist. The soil should be **fertile, humus rich, acidic** and **moist**. Flowering ferns tolerate wet soil and will spread as offsets form at the plant bases.

Tips

These large ferns form an attractive mass when planted in large colonies. They can be included in beds and borders, and make a welcome addition to a woodland garden.

Recommended

O. cinnamomea (cinnamon fern) has light green fronds that fan out in a circular fashion from a central point. Bright green, leafless, fertile fronds that mature to cinnamon brown are produced in spring and stand straight up in the center of the plant. (Zones 2–8)

O. regalis (royal fern) forms a dense clump of foliage. Feathery, fertile, flower-like fronds stand out among the sterile fronds in summer and mature to a rusty brown. **'Purpurescens'** fronds are purple-red when they emerge in spring and mature to green. This contrasts well with the purple stems. (Zones 3–9)

Features: perennial deciduous fern; decorative, fertile fronds; habit **Height:** 2½–5'
Spread: 24–36" **Hardiness:** zones 2–9

Fountain Grass
Pennisetum

P. glaucum 'Purple Majesty'

$\mathcal{F}$ountain grass' low maintenance and graceful form make it easy to place. It will soften any landscape, even in winter.

Growing
Fountain grass thrives in **full sun**. The soil should be of **average fertility** and **well drained**. Plants are drought tolerant once established. Fountain grass may self-seed, but it is not troublesome.

The name Pennisetum alopecuroides *refers to the plumy flower spikes that resemble a fox's tail. In Latin,* penna *means feather, and* seta *means bristle;* alopekos *is the Greek word for fox.*

Shear perennials back in early spring, and divide them when they start to die out in the center.

Tips
Fountain grasses can be used as individual specimen plants, in group plantings and drifts, or combined with flowering annuals, perennials, shrubs and other ornamental grasses. Annual selections are often planted in containers or beds for height and stature.

Recommended
Both perennial and annual fountain grasses exist. Popular perennials include *P. alopecuroides* 'Hameln' (dwarf perennial fountain grass), a compact cultivar with silvery white plumes and narrow, dark green foliage that turns gold in fall, and *P. orientale* (Oriental fountain grass), with tall, blue-green foliage and large, silvery white flowers (zones 6–9, with winter protection).

Annual fountain grasses include *P. setaceum* (annual fountain grass), which has narrow, green foliage and pinkish purple flowers that mature to gray; its cultivar, **'Rubrum'** (red annual fountain grass), which has broader, deep burgundy foliage and pinkish purple flowers; and *P. glaucum* **'Purple Majesty'** (purple ornamental millet), which has blackish purple foliage and coarse, bottlebrush flowers. Its form resembles a corn stalk.

Features: arching, fountain-like habit; silvery pink, dusty rose to purplish black foliage; white, purple flowers; winter interest **Height:** 2–5' **Spread:** 24–36" **Hardiness:** zones 5–9 or grown as an annual

Licorice Plant
Helichrysum

$\mathcal{T}$he silvery sheen of licorice plant is caused by a fine, soft pubescence on the leaves. It is a perfect complement to any plant because silver is the ultimate blending color.

Growing
Licorice plant prefers **full sun**. The soil should be of **poor to average fertility, neutral** or **alkaline** and **well drained**. Licorice plant wilts when the soil dries but revives quickly once watered. If it outgrows its space, snip it back with a pair of pruners, shears or even scissors.

Tips
Licorice plant is a perennial grown as an annual that is prized for its foliage rather than its flowers. Include it in your hanging baskets, planters and window boxes to provide a soft, silvery backdrop for the colorful flowers of other plants. Licorice plant can also be used as a groundcover in beds, borders, rock gardens and along the tops of retaining walls.

Recommended
H. petiolare is a trailing plant with fuzzy, gray-green leaves. Cultivars are more common than the species and include varieties with lime green, silver or variegated leaves.

H. petiolare 'Petite Licorice' (above)
H. petiolare 'Limelight' (below)

Licorice plant is a good indicator plant for hanging baskets. When you see licorice plant wilting, it is time to water your baskets.

Features: trailing habit; colorful, fuzzy foliage
Height: 20" **Spread:** about 36"; sometimes up to 6' **Hardiness:** tender perennial; grown as an annual

Lungwort
Pulmonaria

P. saccharata (above & below)

T he wide array of lungworts have highly attractive foliage that ranges in color from apple green to silver spotted, and olive to dark emerald.

Growing

Lungworts prefer **partial to full shade**. The soil should be **fertile, humus rich, moist** and **well drained**. Rot can occur in very wet soil.

Divide in early summer after flowering or in autumn. Provide the newly planted divisions with a lot of water to help them re-establish.

Tips

Lungworts make useful and attractive groundcovers for shady borders, woodland gardens and pond and stream edges.

Recommended

P. longifolia (long-leaved lungwort) forms a dense clump of long, narrow, white-spotted green leaves and bears clusters of blue flowers.

P. officinalis (common lungwort, spotted dog) forms a loose clump of evergreen foliage, spotted with white. The flowers open pink and mature to blue. Cultivars are available.

P. saccharata (Bethlehem sage) forms a compact clump of large, white-spotted, evergreen leaves and purple, red or white flowers. Many cultivars are available.

To keep lungworts tidy and to show off the fabulous foliage, deadhead the plants by shearing them back lightly after flowering.

Features: decorative mottled foliage; blue, red, pink, white spring flowers **Height:** 8–24" **Spread:** 8–35" **Hardiness:** zones 3–8

Maidenhair Fern

Adiantum

A. *pedatum* (above & below)

These charming and delicate-looking native ferns add a graceful touch to any woodland planting. Their unique habit and texture will stand out in any garden.

Growing

Maidenhair fern grows well in **light or partial shade** but tolerates full shade. The soil should be of **average fertility, humus rich, slightly acidic** and **moist**. This plant rarely needs dividing, but it can be divided in spring to propagate more plants.

Tips

These lovely ferns will do well in any shaded spot in the garden. Include them in rock gardens, woodland gardens, in shaded borders and beneath shade trees.

They also make an attractive addition to a shaded planting next to a water feature or on a slope where the foliage can be seen when it sways in the breeze.

Recommended

A. pedatum forms a spreading mound of delicate, arching fronds. Light green leaflets stand out against the black stems, and the whole plant turns bright yellow in fall. Spores are produced on the undersides of the leaflets.

Also called: northern maidenhair
Features: deciduous perennial fern; summer and fall foliage; habit **Height:** 12–24"
Spread: 12–24" **Hardiness:** zones 2–8

Ostrich Fern
Matteuccia

M. struthiopteris (above & below)

𝒯hese popular, classic ferns are revered for their delicious, emerging spring fronds and their stately, vase-shaped habit.

Growing
Ostrich fern prefers **partial or light shade** but tolerates full shade, or full sun if the soil is kept moist. The soil should be **average to fertile, humus rich, neutral to acidic** and **moist**. Leaves may scorch if the soil is not moist enough. These ferns are aggressive spreaders that reproduce by spores. Unwanted plants can be pulled up and composted or given away.

Tips
This fern appreciates a moist woodland garden and is often found growing wild alongside woodland streams and creeks. Useful in shaded borders, these plants are quick to spread, to the delight of those who enjoy the young fronds as a culinary delicacy.

Recommended
M. struthiopteris (*M. pennsylvanica*) forms a circular cluster of slightly arching, feathery fronds. Stiff, brown, fertile fronds, covered in reproductive spores, stick up in the center of the cluster in late summer and persist through winter. They are popular choices for dried arrangements.

Ostrich ferns are also grown commercially for their edible fiddleheads. The tightly coiled, new spring fronds taste delicious lightly steamed and served with butter. Remove the bitter, reddish brown, papery coating before steaming.

Also called: fiddlehead fern
Features: perennial fern; foliage; habit
Height: 3–5' **Spread:** 12–36" or more
Hardiness: zones 1–8

Pachysandra
Pachysandra

P. terminalis (above & below)

ow-maintenance pachysandra is one of the most popular ground-covers. Its rhizomatous rootzone colonizes quickly to form a dense blanket over the ground.

Growing
Pachysandra prefers **light to full shade** but tolerates partial shade. Any soil that is **moist, acidic, humus rich** and **well drained** is good. These plants can be propagated easily from cuttings or by division.

Tips
Pachysandras are durable groundcovers under trees, in shady borders and in woodland gardens. The foliage is considered evergreen, but winter-scorched shoots may need to be removed in spring. Shear or mow old plantings in early spring to rejuvenate them.

Recommended
P. terminalis (Japanese spurge) forms a low mass of foliage rosettes. It grows about 8" tall and can spread almost indefinitely. **'Variegata'** has white margins or mottled silver foliage, but it is not as vigorous as the species. **'Green Sheen'** has, as its name implies, exceptionally glossy leaves that are smaller than those of the species.

Interplant this popular groundcover with spring bulbs, hostas or ferns, or use it as an underplanting for deciduous trees and shrubs with contrasting foliage colors.

Also called: Japanese spurge
Features: perennial, evergreen groundcover; habit; inconspicuous, fragrant, white, spring flowers **Height:** 8" **Spread:** 12–18" or more
Hardiness: zones 3–8

Reed Grass
Calamagrostis

'Karl Foerster' (above & below)

*T*his is a graceful, metamorphic grass that changes its habit and flower color throughout the seasons. The slightest breeze keeps this grass in perpetual motion.

Growing

Reed grass grows best in **full sun**. The soil should be **fertile, moist** and **well drained**. Heavy clay and dry soils are tolerated. It may be susceptible to rust in cool, wet summers or in areas with poor air circulation. Rain and heavy snow may cause it to flop temporarily, but it quickly bounces back. Cut reed grass back to 2–4" in very early spring before growth begins. Divide the grass if it begins to die out in the center.

Tips

Whether it's used as a single, stately focal point, in small groupings or in large drifts, this is a desirable, low-maintenance grass. It combines well with late-summer and fall-blooming perennials.

Recommended

C. x *acutiflora* 'Karl Foerster' (Foerster's feather reed grass), the most popular selection, forms a loose mound of green foliage from which the airy bottlebrush flowers emerge in June. The flowering stems have a loose, arching habit when they first emerge but grow more stiff and upright over summer. Other cultivars include 'Overdam,' a compact, less hardy selection with white leaf edges. Watch for a new introduction called 'Avalanche,' which has a white center stripe.

If you like how reed grass holds its flowers high above its mounded foliage, consider Deschampsia *(tufted hair grass) and* Molinia *(moor grass) and their species and cultivars. Some have creamy yellow striped foliage.*

Features: open habit becomes upright; silvery pink flowers turn rich tan; green foliage turns bright gold in fall; winter interest
Height: 3–5' **Spread:** 24–36"
Hardiness: zones 4–9

Sensitive Fern
Onoclea

O. sensibilis (above & below)

A common sight along stream banks and in wooded areas of Pennsylvania, this native fern thrives in moist and shaded conditions.

Growing
Sensitive fern grows best in **light shade** but tolerates full or partial shade. The fronds can scorch if exposed to too much sun. The soil should be **fertile, humus rich** and **moist**, though some drought is tolerated. These plants are sensitive to frost and can be easily damaged by late or early frosts.

Tips
Sensitive ferns like to live in damp, shady places. Include them in shaded borders, woodland gardens and other locations with protection from the wind.

Recommended
O. sensibilis forms a mass of light green, deeply lobed, arching fronds. Fertile fronds are produced in late summer and persist through winter. The spores are produced in structures that look like black beads, which give the fertile fronds a decorative appearance that makes them a popular addition to floral arrangements.

Features: deciduous perennial fern; attractive foliage; habit **Height:** 24" **Spread:** indefinite **Hardiness:** zones 4–9

Sweet Potato Vine
Ipomoea

This vigorous, rambling, annual plant with lime green, bruised purple or green, pink and cream variegated leaves can make any gardener look like a genius.

Growing
Grow sweet potato vine in **full sun**. Any type of soil will do but a **light, well-drained** soil of **poor fertility** is preferred.

Tips
Sweet potato vine is a great addition to mixed planters, window boxes and hanging baskets. In a rock garden it will scramble about, and along the top of a retaining wall it will cascade over the edge. Although this plant is a vine, its bushy habit and colorful leaves make it a useful foliage plant.

Recommended
I. batatas (sweet potato vine) is a twining climber that is grown for its attractive foliage rather than its flowers. Several cultivars are available.

'Blackie' (above), 'Margarita' (below)

As a bonus, when you pull up your plant at the end of summer, you can eat any tubers (sweet potatoes) that have formed, or store the dry tubers in a bin to plant the next year.

Features: decorative foliage **Height:** about 12" **Spread:** up to 10' **Hardiness:** grown as an annual

Sweet Woodruff

Galium

Sweet woodruff is a groundcover with abundant, good qualities: attractive, light green foliage that smells like new-mown hay; profuse white spring flowers; and the ability to fill in garden spaces without taking over.

Growing

This plant prefers **partial shade**. It will grow well, but will not bloom well, in full shade. The soil should be **humus rich, slightly acidic** and evenly **moist**. Sweet woodruff competes well with other plant roots and does well where some other groundcovers, like vinca, fail to thrive.

Tips

Sweet woodruff makes a fast-spreading woodland groundcover. It forms a beautiful green carpet and loves the same conditions in which azaleas and rhododendrons thrive. Interplant it with spring bulbs for a fantastic display in spring.

Recommended

G. odoratum is a low, spreading groundcover. It bears clusters of star-shaped, white flowers in a flush in late spring, and these continue to appear sporadically through mid-summer.

G. odoratum (above & below)

Sweet woodruff's vanilla-scented dried leaves and flowers were once used to scent bed linens and were often added to potpourri. They are also used to flavor beverages, particularly the traditional German May wine.

Features: deciduous perennial groundcover; white, late-spring to mid-summer flowers; fragrant foliage; habit **Height:** 12–18" **Spread:** indefinite **Hardiness:** zones 3–8

Switch Grass
Panicum

P. virgatum cultivar (above)
P. virgatum 'Heavy Metal' (below)

Switch grass' delicate, airy panicles can fill gaps in the garden border and can be cut for fresh or dried arrangements.

A native to the prairie grasslands, switch grass naturalizes equally well in an informal border and a natural meadow.

Growing
Switch grass thrives in **full sun, light shade** or **partial shade**. The soil should be of **average fertility** and **well drained**, though the plants adapt to both moist and dry soils and tolerate conditions ranging from heavy clay to lighter sandy soil. Cut switch grass back to 2–4" from the ground in early spring. The flower stems may break under heavy, wet snow or in exposed, windy sites.

Tips
Plant switch grass singly in small gardens, in large groups in spacious borders, or at the edges of ponds or pools for a dramatic, whimsical effect. The seedheads attract birds and the foliage changes color in fall, so place this plant where you can enjoy both features.

Recommended
P. virgatum (switch grass) is suited to wild meadow gardens. Some of its popular cultivars include **'Heavy Metal'** (blue switch grass), an upright plant with narrow, steely blue foliage flushed with gold and burgundy in fall; **'Prairie Sky'** (blue switch grass), an arching plant with deep blue foliage; and **'Shenandoah'** (red switch grass), with red-tinged green foliage that turns burgundy in fall.

Features: clumping habit; green, blue or burgundy foliage; airy panicles of flowers; fall color; winter interest **Height:** 3–5'
Spread: 30–36" **Hardiness:** zones 3–9